BIKEPACKING
WALES

BIKEPACKING WALES

18 MULTI-DAY OFF-ROAD CYCLING ADVENTURES

Emma Kingston

 First published in 2023 by Vertebrate Publishing.

Omega Court, 352 Cemetery Road, Sheffield S11 8FT, United Kingdom.
www.adventurebooks.com

Copyright © 2023 Emma Kingston and Vertebrate Publishing Ltd.

Emma Kingston has asserted her rights under the Copyright, Designs and Patents Act 1988 to be identified as author of this work.

A CIP catalogue record for this book is available from the British Library.

ISBN 978-1-83981-190-6 (Paperback)
ISBN 978-1-83981-191-3 (Ebook)

All rights reserved. No part of this work covered by the copyright herein may be reproduced or used in any form or by any means – graphic, electronic, or mechanised, including photocopying, recording, taping, or information storage and retrieval systems – without the written permission of the publisher.

Front cover: *Riding past Tryfan, Ogwen Valley © RK (route 13).*
Back cover (L–R): *Rhossili Bay (route 01); sunset over the Mawddach Estuary © RK (route 14); Yr Wyddfa (Snowdon) seen from Llyn y Gader © RK (route 13); the Green Bridge of Wales (route 02); descending off Cadair Idris on Ffordd Ddu © RK (route 14).*
Opposite: *Singletrack above the Afon Dysynni © RK (route 14).*
Photography by Emma Kingston and Rob Kingston (© RK) unless otherwise credited.

Maps created by Lovell Johns Ltd. Contains OS data © Crown copyright and database right 2023.
www.lovelljohns.com

Design and production by Jane Beagley, Vertebrate Publishing.

Printed and bound in Europe by Latitude Press.

Vertebrate Publishing is committed to printing on paper from sustainable sources.

Every effort has been made to achieve accuracy of the information in this guidebook. The authors, publishers and copyright owners can take no responsibility for: loss or injury (including fatal) to persons; loss or damage to property or equipment; trespass, irresponsible behaviour nor any other mishap that may be suffered as a result of following the route descriptions or advice offered in this guidebook. The inclusion of a track or path as part of a route, or otherwise recommended, in this guidebook does not guarantee that the track or path will remain a right of way. If conflict with landowners arises we advise that you act politely and leave by the shortest route available. If the matter needs to be taken further then please take it up with the relevant authority.
PLEASE GIVE WAY TO HORSES AND PEDESTRIANS.

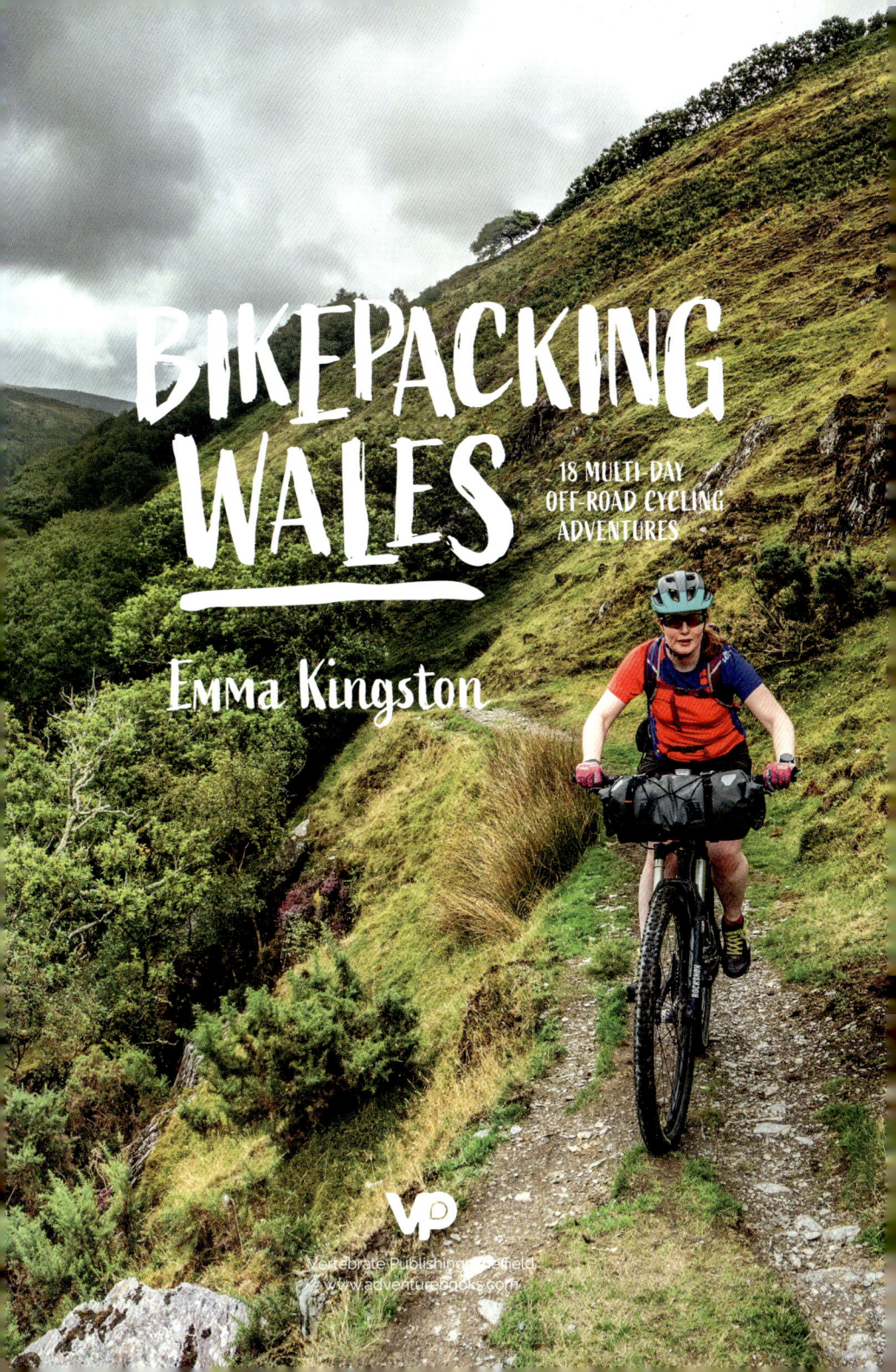

CONTENTS

Introduction vii
Acknowledgements vii
Bikepacking viii
The routes x
Planning your bikepacking trip xi
Wild camping xiv
The Countryside Code xvi
How to use this book xvi
Safety xviii
Further reading xx
The Welsh language xxi

WEST WALES
01 The Gower Peninsula 95.1km/59.1 miles ▲ 3
02 South Pembrokeshire Coast 68.6km/42.6 miles ▲ 11
03 The Preseli Hills 90.6km/56.3 miles ▲ 19

SOUTH WALES & BANNAU BRYCHEINIOG
04 Sarn Helen & the Gap Road 127.8km/79.4 miles ▲ 29
05 The Black Mountains 96.6km/60 miles ▲ 39
06 Cardiff & the Valleys 97.5km/60.6 miles ▲ 47
07 Lower Wye Valley & the Forest Of Dean 95.5km/59.3 miles ▲ 55

MID WALES
08 The Trans Cambrian Way 168.4km/104.6 miles ▲ 65
09 The Elan Valley 109.3km/67.9 miles ▲ 75
10 Mynydd Epynt & the Doethie Valley 122.4km/76.1 miles ▲ 85
11 Shropshire Hills & the Kerry Ridgeway 130.8km/81.3 miles ▲ 95
12 Machynlleth & Nant yr Arian 98.3km/61.1 miles ▲ 103

NORTH WALES & ERYRI
13 Tour of Yr Wyddfa (Snowdon) 95.4km/59.3 miles ▲ 113
14 Tour of Cadair Idris 75.4km/46.9 miles ▲ 123
15 Tour of the Rhinogydd 93.6km/58.2 miles ▲ 131
16 Conwy & the Carneddau 74.1km/46 miles ▲ 139
17 The Triban Trail 163km/101.3 miles ▲ 147
18 Berwyn Hills & the Wayfarer 101.3km/62.9 miles ▲ 155

DOWNLOAD THE BIKEPACKING WALES GPX FILES FROM
www.adventurebooks.com/BPW-GPX

ROUTE GRADES (SEE PAGE XVI)
EASY ▲   MEDIUM ▲   HARD ▲

L–R: *Ty Canol National Nature Reserve* © RK (route 03); *Rhossili Down* (route 01); *Maen Madoc standing stone* © RK (route 04); *limestone pavements above Ystradfellte* © RK (route 04); *Claerwen Reservoir* © RK (route 08); *Conwy Mountain* (route 16).

INTRODUCTION

'It is like that, this country; it takes you over as soon as you set foot in it.'
Raymond Williams, *Border Country* (1960)

Despite growing up in Bristol, I spent most of my childhood weekends and holidays across the border in Wales. We could be on the edge of the Bannau Brycheiniog (Brecon Beacons) National Park in an hour for a walk in the mountains around Abergavenny, mountain biking above Crickhowell, or a day of swimming and waterfall hunting near Ystradfellte. I still recall that sense of excitement as we crossed over the Severn Estuary, passing under the huge mint green towers of what was then called the Second Severn Crossing and pausing at the old toll booths before entering Wales. I love that I still get that same little thrill as an adult.

With this in mind, it is perhaps not surprising that I decided to head to Wales for my first bikepacking trip. I remember spending the evenings leading up to that trip poring over OS maps to concoct a solo adventure around the Elan Valley in Mid Wales, all the while adding to a haphazard pile of cycling kit and old camping gear in the corner of my tiny flat. Despite wrestling with my usual amount of self-doubt, any worries were soon replaced with a growing excitement once I started pedalling. For three wonderful days everything was blissfully simple. I didn't have to think beyond my immediate needs, everything I needed to be self-reliant was strapped to my bike and nothing was more pressing than the present. My feet were constantly wet, the ground still had lingering patches of snow and I spent both nights shivering in a lightweight summer sleeping bag, but I came home utterly elated!

Wales is full of world-class trails and breathtaking scenery, yet it's been the unexpected moments, the half-hidden trails and the surprising encounters that have stood out the most while researching the routes in this book: spending New Year's Eve in front of a bothy fire with a group of mountain biking unicyclists; passing field after field of newborn lambs on the Trans Cambrian Way; and waking in my bivvy bag above a cloud inversion on the Gower Peninsula, with Worm's Head rearing up out of a pure white ocean. Wales can be a challenging place to ride at times, but it has its own indisputable magic.

More than anything, bikepacking in Wales has taught me to read maps like stories, to look for the narrative behind the contours, symbols and place names. In writing this book, I wanted to put together a collection of 18 accessible routes that showcase the Wales that I know and love. Each one reflects both the diversity of Wales's off-road riding and the country's rich culture, history and language. The result is a selection of bikepacking trips which all offer up something slightly different, and I believe that there is a route in this book for everyone who enjoys riding their bike off the beaten track. You'll certainly get to know Wales better as a result.

Croeso i Gymru!
Welcome to Wales!

Emma Kingston
Bristol, March 2023

FEEDBACK AND UPDATES

If you have any feedback, please do contact me: *emmakingstonoutdoors@gmail.com* or *@emma.outdoors*

ACKNOWLEDGEMENTS

My thanks first go to the wonderful team at Vertebrate Publishing – especially Jon Barton, John Coefield, Kirsty Reade, Jane Beagley and Helen Parry – who have helped make both *Bikepacking England* and *Bikepacking Wales* a reality. I would also like to thank Neelke and the team from Snowdonia Mountain Lodge for their generosity and kindness, as well as the friendly Alpkit bike mechanics in Betws-y-Coed for their emergency repairs. Tom Hutton's guidebook *Wales Mountain Biking* has been a huge source of inspiration for my riding over many years too. The Welsh Language Commissioner's list of standardised Welsh place names has been a helpful resource to hopefully ensure that the Welsh language is represented as accurately as possible in this book.

Thanks of course go to my family too. Steve, thank you especially for your company on the Rhinogydd (Rhinogs) – the conditions were dire, but the chat was great. Dad, thank you for generously sharing your photos and support once again, and Mum for gamely coming along on some of my more questionable reconnaissance rides. Finally, I would like to thank my wonderful husband Will. Thank you for your love, support and understanding, especially during the writing process, and for patching me up on the Preseli Hills after what will forever be known as the Hula Hoop Debacle.

BIKEPACKING

Call it what you like – bicycle touring, adventure cycling, bikepacking – these are all different names for what is fundamentally the same thing. At its core, bikepacking is all about getting on a bike and going on an adventure. Pioneering cyclists have been doing exactly that for years, well before the term 'bikepacking' was coined – a look through *The Rough-Stuff Fellowship Archives* comes highly recommended – but the sport has seen an explosion in popularity in recent years.

However, like most broad definitions, the reality is a little more nuanced. Bikepacking as a term has arguably developed over time and is used in this book to describe a style of adventure riding which is self-supported, largely off-road and which incorporates the same type of fun trails you would normally choose for a day out mountain biking. This gives riders the freedom to explore remote landscapes and less-ridden trails which are often only accessed by backpackers on multi-day hikes, and camp out along the way.

ENVIRONMENTAL STEWARDSHIP

With bikepacking growing in popularity and more people seeking out our natural spaces than ever before, it has never been more important to promote respect for the outdoors and to help people get outside responsibly and sustainably. The good news is that the pace of travel (and time in the saddle) while bikepacking allows you to really engage with your surroundings by providing opportunities to learn more about Wales's history, meet local people and their communities, sample Welsh produce and explore places off-route. Wild camping continues this immersion on an even greater scale. As Wendell Berry put it, 'people exploit what they have merely concluded to be of value, but they defend what they love'. You can find more information on wild camping, 'leave no trace' principles and responsible riding on page xiv.

BIKEPACKING IN WALES

'Brooded over by mist, more often than swirled about by cloud … lies the damp, demanding and obsessively interesting country called by its own people Cymru, and known to the rest of the world, if it is known at all, as Wales.'   Jan Morris, *The Matter of Wales* (1984)

Considering the country's size, Wales has an incredibly rich history and is made up of remarkably diverse and contrasting landscapes. Come riding here and you might experience craggy mountains, deep valleys, expansive moorland, peat bogs, rolling fields, ancient woodland, limestone pavements, pristine beaches and miles of varied coastline, possibly all in the same day.

Nearly half of Wales's coastline is designated as a Heritage Coast, and around a quarter of the country lies either within one of its three national parks – Eryri (Snowdonia), Bannau Brycheiniog (Brecon Beacons) and the Pembrokeshire Coast – or one of its five Areas of Outstanding Natural Beauty (AONBs): Llŷn Peninsula, the Clwydian Range and Dee Valley, the Gower Peninsula, Anglesey (Ynys Môn) and the Wye Valley. All of this makes Wales an incredibly scenic place to ride, but often a very hilly place too. On most rides you will need to be prepared to spend a considerable amount of time climbing or pushing.

However, the country's mountainous terrain does offer the key characteristics that many look for when bikepacking: remote trails, more animals than people, a landscape which appears untouched by humans, and a sense of openness and solitude. It is no secret why Wales – Mid Wales in particular – has gained a fast-growing reputation as one of the best bikepacking destinations in the UK. Bear Bones Bikepacking hosts the annual Welsh Ride Thing here – a social, non-competitive multi-day event that has helped introduce many riders to the fun of bikepacking (*www.bearbonesbikepacking.co.uk*) – and Grinduro Wales, a gravel and enduro-style race and bike festival, also takes place near Machynlleth.

There are already several popular long-distance routes in Wales, including: Lôn Las Cymru, a 380-kilometre route from Holyhead to Cardiff; the Wales Coast 2 Coast (also known as Sarn Helen), a 430-kilometre off-road route between Conwy and Worm's Head; The Racing Collective's WalesDURO, a 300-kilometre self-supported race from Bangor to Cardiff; and the Blaenau 600 organised by Epic Cycles. CyclingUK has also created the 225-kilometre Traws Eryri in partnership with Natural Resources Wales (launching summer 2023). However, although these routes make for some fantastic bikepacking trips, not everyone wants to tackle hundreds of kilometres, especially over fairly unforgiving terrain, or can take the necessary time off to complete them. The 18 adventures in this book prove that routes do not need to always be epic in length to give a truly memorable bikepacking adventure around Wales.

A BRIEF HISTORY OF WALES'S OLD ROADS

'Some of the best of cycling would be missed if one always had to be in the saddle or on a hard road.' W.M. Robinson (aka Wayfarer), *'Over the Top'* (1919)

The roads that criss-cross Wales have a rich heritage that is at the heart of Welsh identity. Knowing a little of the history surrounding these tracks, trods, green lanes, holloways and paths can really add to any bikepacking experience here.

As is so often the case, a good place to start is with the Romans who invaded Britain in AD 43. Southern England was rapidly conquered, but the rugged mountains and valleys that would later become known as Wales proved to be a different matter entirely. It took at least another 25 years to suppress the fiercely resistant Celtic tribes, and, although Wales was part of the Roman Empire for over 300 years, it was never fully conquered. There was still plenty of time for the Romans to establish three permanent main bases in Britain though, including one in Wales at Caerleon (Isca). These were part of an elaborate network of forts, fortresses and settlements which were all connected by a web of carefully constructed Roman roads. Wales's most famous example is Sarn Helen and you can still ride along sections of it, especially around Coelbren in the Bannau (route 04, page 29), Betws-y-Coed (route 13, page 113) and Coed y Brenin (route 15, page 131).

The Romans exploited Wales for its mineral wealth too – particularly gold, copper and lead. However, it wasn't until the 19th and 20th centuries that mining and quarrying really began on an industrial scale, this time for highly prized Welsh coal and slate. Wales is covered in old mining paths, tramways and disused railway tracks, some of which have now been re-opened, like the Slate Trail along Lôn Las Ogwen (route 13, page 113) that passes through Penrhyn Quarry.

All that slate and coal had to be transported somehow, and canal boats proved to be a more effective way than carts to carry much heavier loads into the industrial cities. The Scottish engineer Thomas Telford (nicknamed the 'Colossus of the Roads') left his mark right across Wales in the early 19th century, and some of his most impressive achievements include the enormous aqueducts at Chirk and Pontcysyllte (route 18, page 155) – huge watery roads in the sky which you can take bikes across. Most of the canal towpaths permit cycling too.

And then there are the most evocative of Welsh tracks: the drove roads. These centuries-old tracks were used to walk cattle, sheep, pigs and even geese to markets over the border in England. The lead drover (*porthmon*) would have sought out routes away from the main roads to save paying tolls and to avoid mixing their animals with local herds. Many of these routes are now under tarmac or have fallen out of use, but quite a few still exist. Well-known examples include Bwlch y Rhiwgyr ('Pass of the Drovers', route 15, page 131) and the Kerry Ridgeway (route 06, page 47). Look out for rambling farmhouses at crossroads that would have likely once doubled as old droving inns, wide grass verges for grazing and the telltale cluster of Scots pines that farmers planted to advertise overnight accommodation and shoeing stations for the animals.

THE ROUTES

Bikepacking Wales contains 18 multi-day off-road routes of varying length, technicality and remoteness. The routes are spread across the country's three national parks, as well as numerous Areas of Outstanding Natural Beauty (AONBs) and three World Heritage Sites – all of which are free to visit and ride in. These routes cover the full gamut of off-road biking to be found around the country, from coastal riding and scenic gravel trails to remote singletrack and technical mountain descents.

Many of the 18 routes are perfect for an overnight trip that can be squeezed into a weekend. Some lend themselves to shorter, relaxed 'microadventures', like those around Cardiff (route 06, page 47) and the Wye Valley (route 07, page 55). A few of the routes are significantly more substantial and would benefit from being split over multiple days, such as the well-established and popular Trans Cambrian Way (route 08, page 65) and the less well-known Triban Trail (route 17, page 147). While some are linear A-to-B rides, the majority of the routes are loops designed to incorporate an area's best trails, scenery and sites.

Each route offers up a different sort of bikepacking experience. Gower (route 01, page 3) and the South Pembrokeshire Coast (route 02, page 11) each gives riders an unforgettable coastal adventure around spectacular peninsulas, sea cliffs and golden beaches. The Elan Valley (route 09, page 75) in Mid Wales is a bikepacker's paradise with its remote, lonely trails, sprawling reservoirs and numerous bothies. A number of routes incorporate classic mountain biking descents such as the Gap Road (route 05, page 39) and the Doethie Valley (route 10, page 85), while two routes (13 and 14, pages 113 and 123) include optional hike-a-bike ascents of Wales's most iconic peaks – Yr Wyddfa (Snowdon) and Cadair Idris. To the east, the Berwyn Hills (route 18, page 155) offer a quieter, but no less challenging alternative to neighbouring Eryri (Snowdonia) National Park.

The routes are also steeped in Welsh history. Much of the heritage of Wales is tangible: ride under the imposing walls of Conwy Castle (route 16, page 139) and Harlech Castle (route 15, page 131), two of the country's 427 castles that are still standing, trace the story of Owain Glyndŵr and his fight for Welsh independence around Machynlleth (route 12, page 103), and explore the trails around the Valleys (route 06, page 47) and Yr Wyddfa (route 13, page 113) that would have once echoed with the sound of mining and quarrying on an industrial scale. The Preseli Hills (route 03, page 19), meanwhile, are the source of Stonehenge's famous 'bluestones'. Crossed by the Golden Road, these atmospheric hills are covered in prehistoric sites including Pentre Ifan burial chamber – Wales's most impressive megalithic monument.

MOUNTAIN BIKING TRAIL CENTRES

Wales was the birthplace of the UK trail centre phenomenon back in the 1990s, and it continues to lead the way with an ever-expanding network of purpose-built trails across the country. While the routes in this book predominantly use natural bridleways and byways, nine of the routes incorporate short sections of man-made trails. These are mainly blue-graded flow trails with few technical features, and they have been carefully chosen to still be enjoyable when ridden without suspension and on a loaded bike. However, all of these man-made trails can be easily avoided if needed.

Some large trail centres like those at Coed y Brenin (route 15, page 131) – Britain's first purpose-built mountain biking trail centre – and the Forest of Dean (route 07, page 55) offer cyclists a range of amenities including cafes, showers and bike shops, while others like Clyne Valley Woods (route 01, page 3) and Coed Nercwys (route 17, page 147) have little more than an information board and trail map. The man-made trails included in these routes are free to ride but consider helping out on a local dig day or spending a little money on site to help go towards the upkeep and development of the trail network in lieu of car parking fees.

Check online for status updates about trail conditions and closures at trail centres before travelling. More helpful information can be found at *www.mbwales.com/mountain-bike-trails/trail-updates*

PLANNING YOUR BIKEPACKING TRIP
THE BIKE

It is a recurring bikepacking mantra, but it's true: the best bike for bikepacking is the one you already have. It is even better if it is one that you feel comfortable riding on multiple consecutive days. Broadly speaking, full-suspension bikes can provide a more comfortable and enjoyable ride over rougher terrain – almost a given when riding in Wales – but the complexity of the frame adds weight and possible durability concerns. Remember to increase the air pressure in your suspension to compensate for the added weight of your bikepacking bags. A hardtail is arguably the best compromise between speed, comfort and versatility on the more challenging red- and black-graded routes in this book, plus the main frame triangle offers greater space for frame bags or water bottles.

A gravel or adventure bike with drop bars, meanwhile, is going to be considerably faster on the disused railways, forestry tracks and road sections along these routes. Consider opting for flared handlebars to increase the storage capacity of your handlebar bag and think carefully about your tyre and gearing choices. The fairly smooth, mellow trails on the South Pembrokeshire Coast (route 03, page 19) and around Cardiff and the Valleys (route

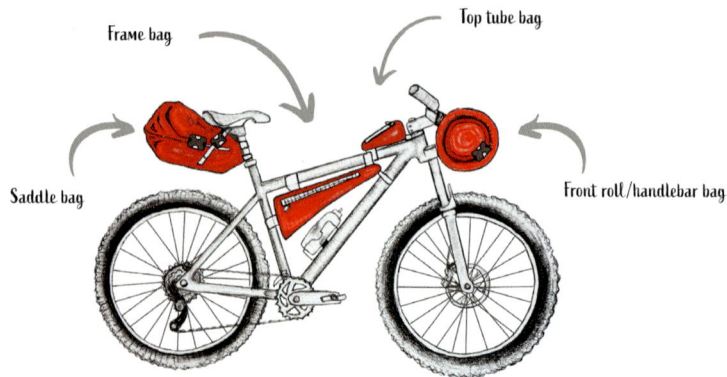

BIKEPACKING KIT LIST
- Shelter (see page xv)
- Sleeping bag & liner
- Air mattress
- Headtorch
- Waterproof jacket
- Stove, fuel & lighter
- Cooking pot & eating utensils
- Food
- Water bottle/hydration bladder
- Water treatment
- First aid kit
- Personal medication
- Essential toiletries
- Bag for rubbish
- Trowel
- Map & compass
- Money (cards & cash)
- External battery pack for charging devices
- Bike lights
- Puncture repair kit
- Spares, tools & pump

EXTRAS
- Spare clothes
- Camera
- Additional water storage
- Camp shoes
- Swim wear
- Travel towel
- Lightweight bike lock

06, page 47), the Wye Valley and the Forest of Dean (route 07, page 55), and Conwy (route 16, page 139) are well suited to these rigid, lighter bikes. Whichever bike you choose, make sure it is in good condition and that you know how to fix common problems before setting off, and remember to check the bike over at the start of each day's riding.

WHAT TO PACK
Just like backpacking, there are weight-conscious bikepackers out there determined to shave every possible gram off their set-up.

It is an admirable goal – the lighter your set-up, the more responsive your bike and the more you will enjoy the riding – although what is considered 'essential' will vary from rider to rider. A pillow? Coffee filter? Spare socks? Experience teaches you which items you are prepared to go without, and tinkering with your set-up is all part of the fun.

When it comes to food, discard any extra bulky packaging to save space. Consider your food's weight-to-calorie ratio and pack dehydrated meals which just need boiling water. Water will add considerable weight to any set-up, but it is one of the most important things not to compromise on. Check available water sources before starting out, refill at every opportunity (if safe to do so) and always know how far away your next water source is. There are usually a number of pubs, cafes, friendly farms or natural water sources to fill up from along the routes in this guidebook, although these cannot always be guaranteed. Some of the routes have very limited amenities, though, and require riders to be almost completely self-sufficient.

The easiest way to stay comfortable on a bikepacking trip is to follow a layering system and choose fabrics that will wick the sweat away from your body and dry quickly. Bring a waterproof, a warm insulated jacket and a hat for the evenings. Padded shorts are highly recommended, as are waterproof mountain biking shorts and cycling gloves. An air mattress creates space between the cold ground and your body while camping and, when paired with a warm three-season sleeping bag and liner, it can be possible to camp throughout the year. Finally, flat mountain biking pedals and shoes can offer more flexibility than clipless pedals and shoes if you intend to explore off-route or need to push your bike for any amount of time.

CARRYING YOUR KIT

There is no right or wrong way to carry your gear. A lot of riders use a combination of bikepacking-specific soft bags which attach directly on to the bike, along with racks for front and rear panniers, rucksacks, hip packs and trailers. It is amazing what you can do with a couple of dry bags and some bungy cords or Voile straps too – bikepacking doesn't have to cost the earth.

Each type of set-up has its pros and cons which will be influenced by your choice of bike and preferred style of riding. For the majority of routes in this guidebook, soft bags are recommended. They require you to pack light, spread the weight well across the bike, and are much less likely to catch on rocks and vegetation either side of narrow trails. Consider using a handlebar bag or harness and a saddle bag for the bulk of your kit, and smaller bags on your top tube and stem to store snacks and accessories for quick access while riding. A frame bag is a good way to store heavier items – depending on the geometry and size of your frame triangle – and helps lower your centre of gravity.

LOGISTICS

These routes can be ridden in any direction, but the suggested trips have been designed so that the best singletrack is usually ridden in descent and that most of the climbs are achievable even on a loaded bike. Each route is accompanied by additional information such as suggestions about water access, supply points, accommodation, points of interest and percentage of off-road riding – some tarmac is inevitable.

The time a route will take will vary from rider to rider. It is worth taking into account your fitness and level of experience, the route distance and elevation, weather and trail conditions, water supplies and hours of daylight, amongst other considerations. Suggested shortcuts and extensions are also included for each route.

Your transport and accommodation choices will influence how you decide to split each route. The start and end points are given as a suggestion only, yet the routes make use of public transport where possible – 14 of the routes start and finish at a train station. If you do need to drive, leave your vehicle somewhere safe overnight (preferably on a well-lit street) and make sure to park considerately if in a residential area.

Different train operators have different bike policies, so it is always best to check if you need to book a space before buying your ticket (as far in advance as possible and at least 24 hours before you travel). Bike reservations are free but limited. On services without reservations, bike spaces are available on a first come, first served basis and are often limited to two bicycles. Some Valleys and Cardiff local routes don't have any space for bikes during peak hours.

ACCOMMODATION

This guidebook features details of purpose-built campsites on or near to each route. Many of these are 'back to basics' sites with rudimentary facilities, while other sites have glamping yurts, small shops and laundry facilities. Be aware that some campsites are seasonal. It is worth noting too that for a small annual fee, membership to the Backpackers Club provides you with access to their UK Farm Pitch Directory: www.backpackersclub.co.uk

Bothies are another great option for bikepacking. These unlocked shelters are free to use and are found in remote locations around the UK, although they can get busy at weekends. Most, but not all, are looked after by the Mountain Bothies Association (MBA); they manage nine bothies in Wales, including Grwyne Fawr bothy (route 05, page 39), Nant Syddion bothy (route 12, page 103) and Penrhos Isaf bothy (route 15, page 131). Visit www.mountainbothies.org.uk to find out their locations and learn more about the Bothy Code, a simple code of conduct which helps make their use sustainable and fair.

Camping barns, bunkhouses, youth hostels and B & Bs are also worth considering, while mountain huts owned by caving, climbing and mountaineering clubs sometimes allow non-members to stay too. Finally, the budget hotel chain Premier Inn has a very friendly bike policy.

WILD CAMPING

Staying in pre-booked accommodation can be a great option when bikepacking, but wild camping often feels like the natural choice after a day's riding. Sometimes it is the only choice available on multi-day bikepacking trips without a substantial detour off-route.

WILD CAMPING LEGALITIES

Although wild camping is broadly legal in Scotland, this is not the case in Wales or across the border in England. Wild camping is not permitted unless you have the permission of the landowner. However, a discreet camp is often possible, especially if you arrive late and leave early. In upland areas such as Eryri (Snowdonia), there has been a long tradition of wild camping and the national park gives clear guidance on its website (www.snowdonia.gov.wales/visit/plan-your-visit/camping). Any camping should be done responsibly and discreetly in the hills and mountains and should follow the Eryri (Snowdonia) Wild Camping Code. In particular, camp high and off the beaten track on open hills and fells, and well away from houses and farms.

More common sense is needed in South Wales which is much more heavily populated, as well as near the border which is a predominantly farmed landscape with fewer opportunities to wild camp out of sight – especially in a tent. Having said that, it is often possible to camp inconspicuously in secluded woodlands, behind hedges and on quiet hilltops. If there are signs asking you not to camp, please do follow them, and wherever you pitch remember that the landowner has the right to ask you to move on.

Do not wild camp along these routes without first attempting to seek the landowner's permission.

LEAVE NO TRACE

If you do choose to wild camp, make sure to follow 'leave no trace' principles to minimise your impact on the land. Pick a durable surface to camp on away from any livestock. Use a camping stove, even if there is evidence that fires have been lit by previous visitors, and seek to draw the least attention to yourself by keeping noise to a minimum and camping in small groups. Make use of public toilets wherever possible, otherwise bury human waste well away from any water sources in a

Camping in the Ogwen Valley (route 13).

hole at least 15 centimetres deep and cover over with turf. Carry out everything you carried in – bag up toilet paper, sanitary products and food waste including biodegradable banana skins, apple cores and orange peel.

These principles extend to riding too. Think about your impact on the trails; try to ride through puddles rather than around them, stick to well-draining bridleways in the wetter months, avoid cutting corners, leave gates as you found them – as per the Countryside Code (page xvi) – and give your tyres a good scrub after a ride to prevent the spread of plant and animal diseases. Even better, go further and try to leave these areas in a better condition than you found them. Consider supporting local mountain biking advocacy groups which often organise trail maintenance days, as well as national campaigns such as Mend Our Mountains and Trash Free Trails.

TYPES OF SHELTERS

Bikepackers have three main options when it comes to their camping set-up: a lightweight tent, a bivvy bag or a tarp. Which you decide to pack will depend on how light and fast you want to travel and how comfortable you like to be, as well as weather conditions and the type of landscape you are riding through. Broadly speaking, a tent is often the slightly heavier option, it takes time to set up and can make you more conspicuous, but it does provide a heightened sense of security and offers better shelter from the elements.

A bivvy bag, meanwhile, is a more discreet and minimalist shelter that offers an additional layer of protection for you and your sleeping bag. Robert Louis Stevenson understood the bivvy bag's appeal back in 1878, writing in *Travels with a Donkey in the Cévennes* that, 'A sleeping-sack ... is always ready – you have only to get into it ... and it does not advertise your intention of camping out to every curious passer-by.' Pairing a bivvy bag with a tarp increases your overnight options and adds little in the way of extra weight.

WILD CAMPING TIPS

Wild camping is often a wonderfully liberating way to spend the night on bikepacking trips, but it can be an intimidating prospect for beginners, even if you are a seasoned mountain biker. For your first experience camping wild, it is a good idea to go on a short overnight trip – preferably during dry, warm weather – to try out your new gear. Consider going with an experienced friend, eating at a pub for dinner or even opting to leave the bike at home.

Finding the ideal place to camp off the beaten track takes practice. While this guidebook does not recommend specific places to wild camp, there are a number of ways to find promising spots. Ordnance Survey (OS) maps are a good place to start to identify features such as buildings, boggy ground, sheltered crags, water sources and types of vegetation on the ground. Satellite images and Google Street View come into their own too once you have homed in on an area, as well as the Geograph® project (*www.geograph.org.uk*) which aims to collect geographically accurate photos and information for every square kilometre of Great Britain and Ireland. It is also a good idea to have a few locations in mind before setting off, and, once there, to take the time to decide on a spot that feels right to you.

THE COUNTRYSIDE CODE
RESPECT EVERYONE
- be considerate to those living in, working in and enjoying the countryside
- leave gates and property as you find them
- do not block access to gateways or driveways when parking
- be nice, say hello, share the space
- follow local signs and keep to marked paths unless wider access is available

PROTECT THE ENVIRONMENT
- take your litter home – leave no trace of your visit
- do not light fires and only have BBQs where signs say you can
- always keep your dogs under control and in sight
- dog poo – bag it and bin it in any public waste bin or take it home
- care for nature - do not cause damage or disturbance

ENJOY THE OUTDOORS
- check your route and local conditions
- plan your adventure – know what to expect and what you can do
- enjoy your visit, have fun, make a memory

HOW TO USE THIS BOOK
ROUTE GRADES
Each of the bikepacking routes in this book has been graded either blue, red or black. These grades differ slightly from those found at UK trail centres, which tend to refer specifically to the level of technical off-road skills required and the obstacles that riders will encounter. Instead, the grades given here consider a number of different factors including route length, elevation, technicality, remoteness and navigation. As ever, these grades are subjective. How you find a particular route will be dictated by your own levels of fitness and skill. Even a straightforward blue-graded route can become a much more serious undertaking if ridden in the winter or if the weather turns foul.

EASY ▲
These routes are a great introduction to bikepacking, suitable for most fitness and skills levels.

MEDIUM ▲
These routes are suitable for riders with good fitness and riding skills.

HARD ▲
These routes are suitable for riders with very good fitness and expert riding skills.

NAVIGATION & ACCURACY

Rather than providing detailed turn-by-turn directions, you can find information on any challenging navigational sections alongside the main text, as well as an introduction to each new area and a short route overview to help you get a feel for the overall trip.

The GPX files provided (see page v) can be easily uploaded on to a GPS device or smartphone to aid with navigation. They are intended to be used in conjunction with a detailed topographical map. Ordnance Survey (OS) maps are the most commonly used and are available as a mobile app; OS Explorer maps (1:25,000) clearly display rights of way. It is always a good idea to carry a paper OS map of the area as a backup too.

While every effort has been made to ensure accuracy within the directions and descriptions in this guidebook, things change and we are unable to guarantee that every detail will be correct. The route conditions might have changed – a large storm could have washed out or blocked trails, while forestry works might have churned up large sections of track, making progress much slower than expected. Wind farm developments in Wales are resulting in the creation of new access tracks that may not be marked on OS maps. The routes in this book are guides only and must be planned and ridden with caution. Please treat stated distance and elevation as guidelines and exercise caution if a direction or part of a GPX file appears at odds with the route on the ground. A comparison between the route description, GPX file and a map should see you on the right track.

RIGHTS OF WAY

Countryside access in Wales has not been particularly kind to cyclists or horse riders, although things are slowly improving. Cyclists in Wales have 'right of way' on bridleways and byways; however, having 'right of way' means 'right of passage', not priority over other traffic – so please ride considerately and give way to walkers and horse riders. Never pass on the inside of a horse, call out early to give the horse and rider time to react and remember to 'Be Nice, Say Hi!'.

Cyclists are also allowed to ride on green lanes and some unclassified roads – although the only way to determine which are legal to ride on and which are not is to check the local authority's definitive map – as well as on any of the forestry roads within the woodlands managed by Natural Resources Wales. Everything else is out of bounds unless, of course, the

MAP KEY

 Route line

 Shortcut/optional route line

 Historic site

 Point of interest

 Mountain bike centre

 Wild swimming

 River crossing

 Camping/campsite

 Accommodation

 Bothy

 Mainline railway

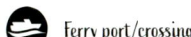 Heritage railway

 Ferry port/crossing

Military firing area

Entry fee

landowner says otherwise. Riding illegally can upset walkers, who have every right to enjoy their day, and is in many cases technically classed as trespass – meaning you could be liable for any damage caused.

Access rights to concessionary or permissive rights of way may be withdrawn at any time so please obey any signs on the ground.

ACCESS REFORMS

The Welsh Government began a consultation on improving access to the outdoors back in 2015, and in the same year Cycling UK and Open MTB launched the 'Trails for Wales' campaign which gained huge public support. In 2019, the Welsh Government announced their intention for significant reforms to public access legislation that would allow cyclists and horse riders increased access to both the rights of way network and to open access land – reforms that had the potential to be 'the most significant changes to rights of way legislation since Scotland's Land Reform Act', according to Duncan Dollimore, head of campaigns for Cycling UK. Unfortunately, the long-awaited report published in 2021 didn't offer the bold recommendations many hoped for. Find out more about the ongoing Trails for Wales campaign at *www.cyclinguk.org*

SAFETY

The ability to read a map, navigate in poor visibility and to understand weather warnings is essential. Don't head out in bad weather unless you're confident and capable of doing so. The Mountain Weather Information Service (MWIS) provides weather forecasts to aid mountain safety for ten upland regions across the UK, including Bannau Brycheiniog (Brecon Beacons) and Eryri (Snowdonia) national parks: *www.mwis.org.uk*

Quite a few of these routes are very remote, cross challenging terrain and are a long way from any kind of shelter. When bikepacking in an upland environment, it is best to think more like a mountaineer than a cyclist in terms of clothing and equipment. The uplands of Wales have on average more than 50 days of rain during the winter months, and there is snow on the summit of Yr Wyddfa (Snowdon) for an average of 30 days a year.

A number of the routes in this book have tough climbs and steep descents that can be hazardous. Ride within your limits, especially if riding solo. If you do choose to ride alone, think about the seriousness of an accident – you might be without help for a very long time. Tell someone where you are going, what time you expect to be back and what time they should ring emergency services if they haven't heard from you. Take a mobile phone, but don't expect a signal. A satellite communication device is a great safety investment to consider as it allows you to send and receive messages regardless of phone signal.

Build in some contingency options in case your trip doesn't go according to plan by identifying bail-out options and alternative roads or trails. Remember to keep reapplying sun cream on sunny days, eat and drink before you feel you need to, and always wear a helmet.

Dolwyddelan Castle © RK (route 13).

WELSH LANGUAGE GLOSSARY

aber – estuary, confluence, stream
adwy – gap, pass
afon – river
argoed – wood, grove
bach (also fach) – small, little
bala – narrow land between two lakes, outlet of a lake
bedd – grave
betws – chapel
blaen – source of a river or stream
bont (also pont) – bridge
bryn – hill
bwlch – gap, pass
cadair – seat, stronghold
caer – stronghold, fort
capel – chapel
carn – heap of stones
carreg – stone, rock
carnedd – heap of stones, tumulus
castell – castle, small stronghold
cefn – ridge
coch – red
coed – tree
cors – bog
crib – crest, ridge
craig – rock
cwm – valley, dale
dâr – oak
dinas – hill-fortress, city
dôl – meadow
dŵr – water
dyffryn – valley
eglwys – church
esgair – long ridge
fawr (also mawr) – big

IN THE EVENT OF AN ACCIDENT

In the event of an emergency, ring **999** or **112**, ask for **Police** and (depending on which part of Wales you are in) then ask for **Mountain Rescue**. You will need to provide details of your location– a grid reference will speed up their response time.

EMERGENCY RESCUE BY SMS TEXT

Another option is to contact the emergency services by SMS text – this is useful if you have a low battery or intermittent signal. Texts can often get through when a call cannot. Register your phone by texting '**register**' to **999** and follow the instructions. **Do it now** – it could save yours or someone else's life: *www.emergencysms.net*

FURTHER READING

Cycling Lôn Las Cymru by Richard Barrett
Wild Wales by George Borrow
On the Trail of the Welsh Drovers by Twm Elias
The Drovers' Roads of Wales by Fay Godwin and Shirley Toulson
The Beaches of Wales by Alistair Hare
Wales Mountain Biking by Tom Hutton
The Matter of Wales by Jan Morris
Dictionary of the Place-Names of Wales by Hywel Wyn Owen and Richard Morgan
Wild Guide Wales by Daniel Start and Tania Pascoe
Great British Gravel Rides by Markus Stitz
Lost Lanes Wales by Jack Thurston
People of the Black Mountains by Raymond Williams

THE WELSH LANGUAGE

'Even without the contour lines, the icons and the colour coding, the names hold the landscape.'
Dominick Tyler, *Uncommon Ground*, 2015

Welsh (Cymraeg) is one of the oldest living languages in Europe – certainly the oldest in Britain. It is closely related to Cornish and Breton and shares some similarities with other Celtic languages, such as Irish, Scottish Gaelic and Manx. It is a thriving language, having been brought back from the brink after deliberate acts of suppression including Henry VIII's Act of Union in 1536, and the Treason of the Blue Books. Today, as an official language, Welsh is growing in daily usage and the Welsh Government aims to have a million Welsh speakers by 2050.

In many areas in Wales (Cymru), you'll hear Welsh used alongside English, but you don't need to understand a word of Welsh to get by. However, knowing some basic vocabulary can really enhance how you experience your surroundings when on a ride. In Wales, there is a close connection between language and landscape, and the meanings of Welsh place names are often very transparent to Welsh speakers. On these pages is a glossary of some key terms to help with understanding many of the place names mentioned in this book.

Many Welsh places have both English and Welsh names. In this book, I have used both names when first mentioning a place – the most commonly used name is referred to thereafter. However, I have also tried to reflect the growing call to protect, re-emphasise and, in some cases, rediscover Welsh place names. For example, two of Wales's national parks have recently reclaimed their Welsh names: Bannau Brycheiniog (Brecon Beacons) and Eryri (Snowdonia). You will also find Wales's highest peak, Yr Wyddfa (Snowdon), referred to by its Welsh name in this book.

foel (also moel) – bare hill
ffridd – enclosed mountain pasture
ffordd – way, road
glyn – deep valley, glen
hafod – summer dwelling
hendre – winter dwelling
hen – old
isaf – lowest
llan – church, monastery
llanerch – clearing, glade
llech – slab, stone, rock
llwybr – path
llyn – lake
maen – stone
mawn – peat
mynydd (also fynydd) – mountain
nant – brook, dingle, glen
ogof – cave
pant – hollow, valley
pen – head, top, end, edge
pentre – homestead, village
pistyll – spout, waterfall
porth – harbour, bay
pwll – pit, pool
rhaeadr – waterfall
rhiw – hill, slope
rhos – heath, moorland
rhyd – ford
sarn – causeway
traws – cross, traverse
tre (also tref) – settlement, hamlet, town
ty – house
uchaf – upper, highest
ynys – island
ystrad – valley, river-meadow

WEST WALES

01 THE GOWER PENINSULA

INTRODUCTION
The Gower Peninsula (Penrhyn Gŵyr) was the first place in Britain to be designated an Area of Outstanding Natural Beauty, in 1956. Often described as 'Wales in miniature', Gower boasts some of the finest beaches and unspoilt coastal scenery in the UK, including the four-kilometre sweep of golden sand below Rhossili Down, the iconic Three Cliffs Bay and the earliest known human burial site in Western Europe at Paviland Cave. The most dramatic sight, however, is Worm's Head (Pen Pyrod) – a long, rocky tidal island that snakes out into Rhossili Bay. Gower has become increasingly well known for its prized local produce, and a bikepacking trip here wouldn't be complete without sampling Gower's famous salt marsh lamb, cockles, laverbread (Welshman's caviar) or a refreshing pint of Gower Gold.

ROUTE OVERVIEW
Gower has a fast-growing reputation for being one of the best bikepacking destinations in Wales, and justifiably so. For such a compact area, it offers up a huge variety of trails which are made all the more spectacular by their unique coastal location. Highlights along this route include the sandy singletrack by Pennard Castle, ridgeline cruising along heather-clad Cefn Bryn, some surprisingly good purpose-built trails in Clyne Valley Country Park, and the jewel in Gower's crown: Rhossili Down. Climb steeply to enjoy the high-level bridleway running along its entire length or stay low to ride one of the most scenic stretches of singletrack in Wales along the edge of Rhossili Bay. This fairly short route is ideal for a weekend adventure of riding, swimming, camping and exploring, and provides one of the best backdrops for watching the sunset in the UK.

NAVIGATION
The route follows some of the waymarked mountain biking trails in Clyne Valley Country Park. It also makes use of recent changes to the paths across Pennard Golf Club – some have been upgraded to bridleways and others have been diverted: www.swansea.gov.uk/rightsofwaymap

Previous page: *The South Pembrokeshire Coast* © Will Kingston-Budge (route 02). *Bridleway above Rhossili Bay* © RK.

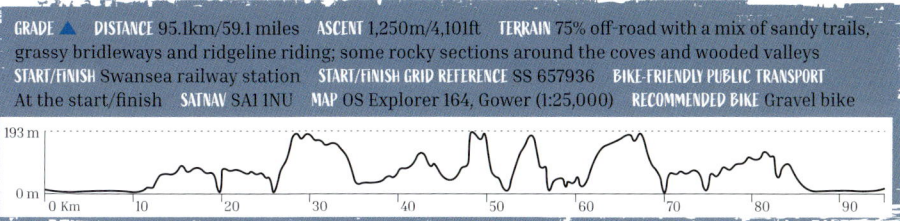

GRADE ▲ **DISTANCE** 95.1km/59.1 miles **ASCENT** 1,250m/4,101ft **TERRAIN** 75% off-road with a mix of sandy trails, grassy bridleways and ridgeline riding; some rocky sections around the coves and wooded valleys **START/FINISH** Swansea railway station **START/FINISH GRID REFERENCE** SS 657936 **BIKE-FRIENDLY PUBLIC TRANSPORT** At the start/finish **SATNAV** SA1 1NU **MAP** OS Explorer 164, Gower (1:25,000) **RECOMMENDED BIKE** Gravel bike

01 THE GOWER PENINSULA

THE ROUTE

'One afternoon, in a particularly bright and glowing August ... George Hooping, whom we called Little Cough, Sidney Evans, Dan Davies, and I sat on the roof of a lorry travelling to the end of the Peninsula ... Inside the lorry were two tents, a box of food, a packing-case of kettles and saucepans and knives and forks, an oil lamp, a primus stove, ground sheets and blankets, a gramophone with three records, and a table-cloth from George Hooping's mother.' Dylan Thomas, *Portrait of the Artist as a Young Dog* (1940)

The Gower Peninsula has long been associated with the famous writer and poet Dylan Thomas. Growing up in nearby Swansea (Abertawe), Thomas regularly referred to himself as a 'townee' rather than a country man, living for 'the provincial drive, the morning café, the evening pub'. But even he was moved by the Gower Peninsula's extraordinary landscape and felt that it was one of the loveliest stretches of coast in the whole of Britain. In one of his semi-autobiographical short stories, Thomas recounts a fortnight-long camping trip on the peninsula where he and his friends travelled along narrow lanes perched on top of a tall lorry, set up their tents in a field overlooking Rhossili Bay and danced around campfires until midnight.

Even as an adult, a bikepacking trip on the Gower Peninsula seems to conjure a similar feeling of childish delight and freedom. Ride crank-deep down through sand dunes, hop over stepping stones and swim across the bays before crawling, exhausted, into a bivvy bag at the end of the day.

Starting at Swansea railway station, the route heads along the Swansea Bike Path and follows the line of the old Mumbles tramway. Swansea was Dylan Thomas's home for more than half his short life – 'this sea-town was my world' – and you can still visit the beautifully restored Georgian house (£) that he grew up in, as well as the Dylan Thomas Centre (free) nearby. Cycling along the smart seafront, it is a world away from the noise and pollution that was generated here during the Industrial Revolution, when the Lower Swansea Valley was for a time the biggest copper processing area in the world. By 1850, 11 major copperworks had been built on the banks of the River

WHEN TO RIDE

Rhossili Down, Llanmadoc Hill and Cefn Bryn are criss-crossed with grassy singletrack which is far more enjoyable when dry, while the woodland trails between the Mumbles and Penmaen can get muddy and churned up after wet weather. Save this trip for a warm spring or summer weekend to make the most of the many ice cream parlours and swimming spots.

WARNINGS

The route joins the B4436 for a short stretch and crosses two golf courses. The trails around Bishopston Valley, Pwlldu Bay and Brandy Cove are wonderfully scenic, but also much steeper and rockier than the rest of the route – you can easily follow the road to Southgate to miss them out if needed. There can be strong tidal rips at Three Cliffs Bay; it is recommended that you swim elsewhere on the peninsula. Worm's Head is only accessible for two and a half hours either side of low tide – check tide times before crossing and only attempt if there is sufficient time to return to the mainland. Visit the National Coastwatch Institution lookout station nearby (grid reference: SS 403874) for further advice.

L–R: *Pennard Castle* © RK; *Arthur's Stone (Maen Ceti)* © RK; *stepping stones at Three Cliffs Bay* © RK; *Pennard Burrows* © RK; *Oxwich Bay.*

WATER
The route is a lot less remote than it feels at times, with village shops, cafes and pubs at regular intervals along the way. There is an outside tap available at the front of the National Trust shop and visitor centre at Worm's Head, next to the car park and toilet block.

FOOD AND DRINK
- Pennard Stores and Post Office, Pennard. T: 01792 233 230
- Little Valley Bakery, Gower Heritage Centre. T: 01792 371 346
- King Arthur Hotel, Reynoldston. T: 01792 390 775
- The Lookout, Rhossili. T: 01792 391 696
- The Bay Bistro, Rhossili. T: 01792 390 519
- Eddy's Cafe Bar, Hillend (seasonal). T: 01792 386 606
- Kings Head Inn, Llangennith. T: 01792 386 212
- Britannia Inn, Llanmadoc. T: 01792 386 624
- Penmaen and Nicholaston Village Hall (SS 525884) runs a coffee and cake morning on the first Saturday of the month (10.30–12.30) – access is through the gate in front of the row of houses by Tor Bay car park.

ACCOMMODATION
- Nicholaston Farm Camping and Caravan Site, Penmaen. T: 01792 371 209
- Three Cliffs Bay Holiday Park, Penmaen. T: 01792 371 218
- Eastern Slade Camp Site, Slade. T: 07970 969 814
- Greenways of Gower, Oxwich. T: 01792 391 203
- YHA Port Eynon. T: 0345 371 9135
- Hillend Caravan & Camping Park, Llangennith. T: 01792 386 204
- Kennexstone Camping and Touring Park, Llangennith. T: 01792 386 790

Tawe, and Swansea quickly became known as 'Copperopolis'. When the copper factories finally closed, they left a wasteland of slag heaps, polluted soil, and foul-smelling smoke laced with sulphur and arsenic, but a huge regeneration project in the 1960s helped reclaim the land and transform the area.

Past Mumbles Head, the route becomes increasingly tranquil, rural and remote as it edges west towards the golf course at Pennard Burrows. Playful, sandy singletrack hugs the edge of the fairway, staying high above a steep wooded valley and passing right under the crumbling walls of Pennard Castle. Down below, the stepping stones across Pennard Pill are just visible as the river meanders across the valley floor in a series of wide, unhurried bends. Past the castle, the bridleway descends down through the sand dunes to reach Three Cliffs Bay; it's more surfing than riding as you fight to stay on your bike in the deep sand.

Turning inland, the route climbs up above Penmaen on to Cefn Bryn Common – the backbone of the peninsula – to join a superb high-level bridleway along the entire ridge. It's so good, it features twice. Riding past prehistoric hut circles, cairns and burial chambers, there are panoramic views north across the open salt marshes of the Loughor Estuary and south over the golden sands of Oxwich Bay. Arthur's Stone (Maen Ceti), one of Wales's most famous prehistoric monuments, lies just off the ridgeline track and is well worth the short detour.

The jewel in Gower's crown, though, comes right at the very end of the peninsula. Criss-crossed with a number of excellent bridleways, Rhossili Down rises above the surrounding landscape like the keel of an upturned boat, looking down over the four-kilometre sweep of Rhossili Bay below. There is a superb natural plunge pool to jump in at low tide at the far end of the beach, in the middle is a shipwreck (the *Helvetia*) to explore, and at its southern end lies iconic Worm's Head, a long, thin, rocky promontory that snakes far out into Rhossili Bay. The name comes from the Norse word *wyrm* meaning 'snake',

which is what its unusual profile must have looked like to Viking sailors. For two and a half hours either side of low tide, you can cross the natural causeway and walk out on to Low Neck and Outer Head, which are connected by the spectacular Devil's Bridge. But note that even locals get caught out; Dylan Thomas once got marooned on Worm's Head as an adult after falling asleep while reading his book.

Looking out across Rhossili Bay, a spectacular stretch of coastal singletrack contours above the beach past a lone white house. This former rectory was used as a base for radar workers during World War II and was almost bought by Thomas for his family until he found out there was no pub in the village. The bridleway along the top of Rhossili Down is even better, although it's a steep push up to reach it; spend the evening watching the sunset over Worm's Head with the ponies, before tucking into a fry-up at Eddy's Cafe Bar the next morning.

The return leg back east to Swansea celebrates both Gower's great riding and the area's long history of good food and drink. Just past the dreamy singletrack on Llanmadoc Hill, 14th-century Weobley Castle is home to famous Gower salt marsh lamb, where the animals graze the marshes on a diet of wild samphire, sorrel, sea lavender and thrift. The Britannia Inn in Llanmadoc and the King Arthur Hotel in nearby Reynoldston have recently been singled out as two of the best pubs in Britain. After a fast descent to Parkmill through dense banks of wild garlic, you pass close to Gower Heritage Centre (£), which is well worth a visit. Based in a restored 12th-century watermill, you can take a self-guided tour around the blacksmith's forge and the woollen mill and watch the last intact and working water wheel on Gower making light work of the local grain. Finally, treat yourself to a pint of Gower Gold in one of the local pubs – the beer is produced by Gower Brewery in Crofty. This is a bikepacking trip that will linger in the memory, long after the last bubbles of foam have burst.

Camping pitches will need to be booked well in advance in the summer, as well as during school holidays and bank holidays. Most sites on the peninsula are seasonal, and there are very few campsites west of Oxwich Bay.

OTHER ROUTES NEARBY
Rather than returning to Swansea, there is the option to follow Sustrans Route 4 westwards instead. It joins the Millennium Coastal Path past Burry Port towards Pembrey Country Park, which hosts the annual Battle on the Beach, a unique cycling event that includes a mass beach start.

BIKE SHOPS AND HIRE
· The Bike Hub, Swansea.
T: 01792 466 944
· Essential Cycles Gower, Parkmill.
T: 07968 705 282

SUPPORT
The Clyne Riders help develop and maintain the waymarked mountain bike trails in Clyne Valley Country Park: www.facebook.com/groups/clyneriders

L–R: *Worm's Head; bivvy view from Rhossili Down.*

02 SOUTH PEMBROKESHIRE COAST

INTRODUCTION
Pembrokeshire (Sir Benfro) is Wales's most westerly county. It juts out into the Celtic Sea and is edged by some of the most dramatic coastline in southern Britain, most of which lies within Pembrokeshire Coast National Park. It is the only national park in the UK to have been designated largely because of its coastline – nowhere within the national park is more than 16 kilometres from the sea. The South Pembrokeshire Coast is renowned for its pristine Blue Flag beaches, as well as its huge vertical sea cliffs. Look out for impressive rock features including deep chasms, huge sea stacks and rock arches, all with evocative names like Huntsman's Leap, the Green Bridge of Wales and the Cauldron. To the north, the coastline is guarded by Pembroke Castle – the birthplace of Henry VII, founder of the Tudor dynasty. Public access along the coast is restricted due to military activity at Castlemartin Firing Range, but when the range is open it feels remarkably empty and remote.

ROUTE OVERVIEW
With its sandy beaches, flat non-technical trails and low mileage, you'd be hard pressed to find a more laid-back bikepacking trip in Wales. This scenic route takes riders on a leisurely tour of Pembrokeshire's south coast, working its way west predominantly on quiet tarmac lanes to explore the Angle Peninsula, home to sandy bays, historic forts and Cafe Môr – an award-winning solar-powered mobile kitchen specialising in seafood and now based at The Old Point House pub. Once past Freshwater West, the route hugs the edge of the cliffs on the Pembrokeshire Coast Path across Castlemartin Firing Range.

NAVIGATION
This is a very straightforward route. The bridleway between Elegug Stacks and Broad Haven is clearly waymarked and follows the edge of the coast. The route also runs parallel with the Castlemartin Range Trail between Gupton Bay and Merrion – providing an off-road option for riders wanting to stay off the tarmac as much as possible. Follow the symbol of a tank inside a green circle.

Pembrokeshire Coast Path
© Will Kingston-Budge.

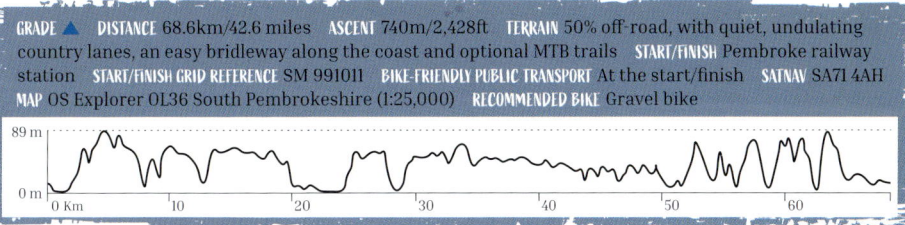

GRADE ▲ **DISTANCE** 68.6km/42.6 miles **ASCENT** 740m/2,428ft **TERRAIN** 50% off-road, with quiet, undulating country lanes, an easy bridleway along the coast and optional MTB trails **START/FINISH** Pembroke railway station **START/FINISH GRID REFERENCE** SM 991011 **BIKE-FRIENDLY PUBLIC TRANSPORT** At the start/finish **SATNAV** SA71 4AH **MAP** OS Explorer OL36 South Pembrokeshire (1:25,000) **RECOMMENDED BIKE** Gravel bike

There are birdwatching and swimming spots galore, as well as plenty of places to explore along the way such as the fun mountain biking trails on the Stackpole Estate, Bosherston Lily Ponds, historic Stackpole Quay and St Govan's Chapel – a tiny hermit's cell wedged in a cleft between the cliffs.

THE ROUTE

Turning down the narrow road into the artillery range, the red flags are lowered, curling limply around their white poles in the absence of any coastal breeze. A row of army vehicles is parked up in a line outside the observation tower. Further on, the rusting shells of two camouflaged tanks poke out behind a grassy bank, while Flimston Chapel sits on its own in the middle of a field. For a second, it looks like the chapel tower is on fire, a burst of pink flames rising from the roof. In the time it takes to do a double take and look back again, the flare has vanished.

The South Pembrokeshire Coast is a land of contrasts and contradictions. It is one of the most restricted outdoor spaces to visit in Wales, yet it contains the longest section of the Pembrokeshire Coast Path National Trail open to cyclists. It is part of Pembrokeshire Coast National Park – designated primarily for its stunning coastline – yet it sits cheek by jowl with the Pembroke Oil Refinery on the industrialised shores of Milford Haven (Aberdaugleddyf), with its huge storage tanks, cooling towers and eerie flares. And it boasts a huge number of peaceful and unspoilt beaches, yet a significant part of the coast is used by the military for intensive large-scale target practice. In spite of these contrasts, and in many ways because of them, this stunning stretch of coastline is a fascinating place to ride, camp and explore.

Perhaps the most obvious contrast though is where the land meets the sea. As you ride along quiet lanes to reach the south of the Castlemartin Peninsula, the fields stretch out in front in a smooth, unbroken plateau. The ocean simply appears to be a continuation of the land. With nothing to fix upon the horizon or provide a sense of scale, there's a feeling of vastness and grandeur which seems at odds with the flat terrain. That is, until you reach the edge. At Flimston Down, the land abruptly

WHEN TO RIDE

This is a short route best enjoyed in the summer. It stays on quiet lanes and hard gravel tracks, but the optional mountain biking trails in the Stackpole Estate are not armoured like the tracks at most Welsh trail centres and can get muddy after wet weather.

WARNINGS

Part of this route crosses Castlemartin Range East and access is restricted at certain times. It is usually open at weekends and public holidays but check before travelling. Timetables are published two months in advance at www.gov.uk/government/publications/castlemartin-firing-notice--2 or call 01646 662 367 from 8.15 a.m. for daily updates and last-minute closures. If the red flags are flying and/or lights are flashing, do not enter the training area. Keep away from all buildings, bunkers and military installations except for Flimston Chapel and St Govan's Chapel, avoid touching objects lying on the ground and stay on the seaward side of the white stakes. If you want to swim, be aware that the sea off West Angle Bay and Freshwater West in particular has very strong currents.

L–R: *Coast around Elegug Stacks* © RK; *St Govan's Country Inn, Bosherston; Broadhaven South Beach* © RK; *warning signs at Castlemartin Firing Range; Bosherston Lily Ponds, Stackpole Estate* © RK.

WATER

There is an outside tap at the toilet block in Broad Haven National Trust car park. Otherwise, there is little access to fresh water – carry what you need or fill up in one of the pubs or cafes en route.

FOOD AND DRINK

- Wavecrest Cafe, Angle. T: 01646 641 457
- The Cookhouse Cafe, Chapel Bay Fort. T: 07437 568 654
- Cafe Môr and The Old Point House, Angle Village. T: 01646 792 100
- Ye Olde Worlde Cafe, Bosherston. T: 01646 661 216
- St Govan's Country Inn, Bosherston. T: 01646 661 311
- The Stackpole Inn, Stackpole. T: 01646 672 324
- The Boathouse Tea Room, Stackpole. T: 01646 623 110

terminates in sheer limestone cliffs with the ocean suddenly 50 metres below, roiling and churning around the area's impressive geological features. At the end of the artillery range road, the famous Green Bridge of Wales arches out of the water next to two huge pillars known as Elegug Stacks. Further east along the coastal bridleway, Flimston Castles headland is well worth exploring too – cross the defensive curving ramparts of an ancient fort to find the Cauldron, a cavernous blowhole that you can walk all the way around and peer into.

In spring and summer, these cliffs are a bristling, noisy sight to ride past, teaming with guillemots, razorbills and rare choughs. The guillemots like to pack together, squeezing in huge numbers on to the narrow ledges, while razorbills – the emblem of the national park – build their nests in crevices in the rock. Castlemartin has the highest concentration of seabirds on the Pembrokeshire mainland, and this is largely due to the continued military presence in the area.

The route crosses Castlemartin Range East which has been used by the Ministry of Defence as a firing range since it was requisitioned in 1938. Further west, the coastline around the Angle Peninsula is dotted with ruined forts and batteries built to defend the Milford Haven waterway from the French and the Spanish, while just across the water you can make out Mill Bay where Henry Tudor landed in 1485, ready to stake his claim to the throne. The route passes right under the imposing walls of Pembroke Castle (Castell Penfro; £), the future king's birthplace and childhood home. 'Harri Tudur' would have been able to draw on his Welsh lineage as he marched through the country, recruiting local men for his army before defeating Richard III at

the Battle of Bosworth and claiming the crown as Henry VII.

Riding east along the coast, the bridleway is broad, flat and grassy, yet never dull. The sea is a hypnotic and constant presence; regular signs remind you of the explosive consequences of straying off the path and, every now and then, a colourful climbing helmet pops up into view. Pembrokeshire's cliffs offer some of the most spectacularly positioned rock climbs in the UK, and riding along the cliff edge you get a sense of what it must feel like to make move after committing move high above the ocean. As Mike Robertson writes in the *Pembroke* guidebook, this area 'epitomises all that our eclectic world of climbing can offer: isolation, wonderment, freedom, space'. Bikepacking here feels much the same. Peer down into the long, narrow chasm known as Huntsman's Leap, ride out to Saddle Head along a strip of concrete lined with pink sea thrift and sea campion, and clamber down the steep stone steps to visit tiny St Govan's Chapel carved out of the limestone cliffs.

As the route works its way east, the sheer cliffs briefly disappear. A new, permissive bridleway passes through a military checkpoint, narrowing to singletrack above Star Rock just before reaching Broad Haven. Leave your bike here to explore the golden bays, sand dunes and secret coves, as well as inland to the Bosherston Lily Ponds and the Mere Pool Valley, all of which can only be accessed on foot. Further inland, Bosherston has a great pub and cafe, the waymarked mountain biking trails in Stackpole Estate are short-lived but good fun and the extensive ruins of the Bishop's Palace (free entry) near Lamphey – once a lavish country retreat for the medieval bishops of St Davids – are well worth visiting too.

ACCOMMODATION
- Gupton Farm Campsite, Castlemartin (two nights minimum stay). T: 01646 661 640
- Parke Farm Camping, Merrion. T: 01646 450 452
- Buckspool Farm Campsite, Bosherston. T: 01646 685 825
- Trefalen Farm Campsite, Bosherston. T: 01646 661 643
- Bosherston Campsite, Bosherston. T: 01646 685 825
- Stackpole Under the Stars, Cheriton (three nights minimum stay in high season). T: 01646 683 167
- Upper Portclew Farm Camping and Caravan Site, Freshwater East. T: 01646 672 112

Camping pitches need to be booked well in advance in the summer, as well as during school holidays and bank holidays.

OTHER ROUTES NEARBY
The Castlemartin Range Trail allows cyclists safe access along the range boundary even when the range is closed to the public. The traffic-free Llwybr Brunel – the Brunel Trail – follows Sustrans Route 4 north-west to Haverfordwest and is part of the long-distance Celtic Trail. If you follow route 4 east instead, it takes you on quiet country lanes to Tenby, one of Wales's most beautiful seaside towns.

BIKE SHOPS AND HIRE
- Bierspool Cycles, Pembroke Dock. T: 01646 681 039

L–R: *Stackpole Head © RK; St Govan's Chapel.*

03 THE PRESELI HILLS

INTRODUCTION
The rugged North Pembrokeshire Coast has a very different feel to the national park's southern edge. Instead of sheer cliffs, the northern coastline is dotted with hundreds of rocky coves nestled between windswept headlands. The far western tip of the North Pembrokeshire Coast is home to the tiny cathedral city of St Davids (Tyddewi), while further east Fishguard (Abergwaun) sits in the shadow of the Preseli Hills (Mynydd Preseli) which rise out of the landscape to 536 metres. Topped with hillforts and rocky tors – some of which supplied the bluestones that now form the inner circle of Stonehenge – these atmospheric hills are steeped in legends from *The Mabinogion* and covered in prehistoric monuments such as Pentre Ifan, one of Wales's best-known ancient sites.

ROUTE OVERVIEW
Walkers are spoilt for choice here, with 299 kilometres of the stunning Pembrokeshire Coast Path to enjoy, but options are much more limited for cycling. Thankfully, North Pembrokeshire boasts a number of superb bridleways and pubs which together make an unforgettable loop of the Preseli Hills. This route takes in some extremely varied riding, including Welsh Water's new purpose-built trails around Llys-y-frân Reservoir, and mossy woodland singletrack in Ty Canol. The highlight of the route, though, is the historic Golden Road – an incredible 11-kilometre bridleway that undulates along the main ridge of the Preseli Hills. Its slow, boggy sections won't be to everyone's taste, but riders who persevere are rewarded with high-level grassy singletrack and panoramic views as far as the Wicklow Mountains in Ireland.

Ty Canol National Nature Reserve © RK.

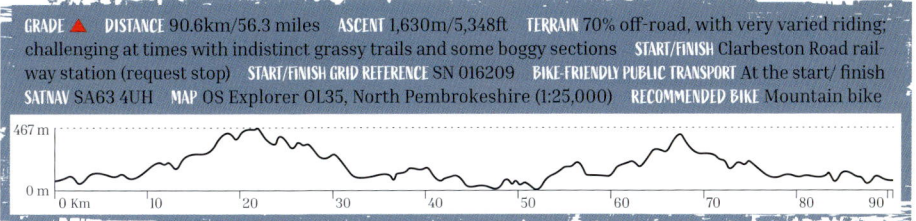

GRADE ▲ DISTANCE 90.6km/56.3 miles ASCENT 1,630m/5,348ft TERRAIN 70% off-road, with very varied riding; challenging at times with indistinct grassy trails and some boggy sections START/FINISH Clarbeston Road railway station (request stop) START/FINISH GRID REFERENCE SN 016209 BIKE-FRIENDLY PUBLIC TRANSPORT At the start/finish SATNAV SA63 4UH MAP OS Explorer OL35, North Pembrokeshire (1:25,000) RECOMMENDED BIKE Mountain bike

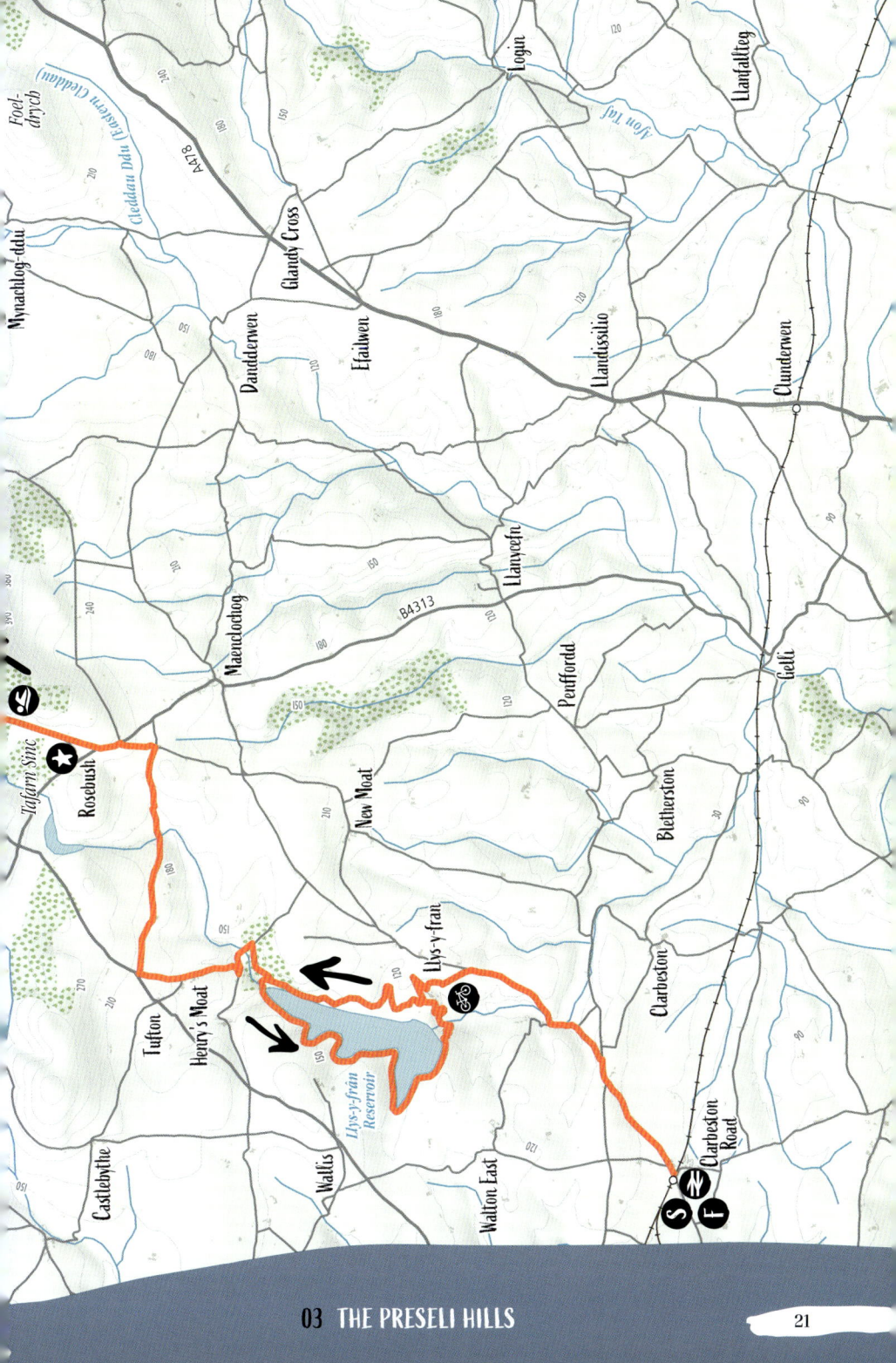

03 THE PRESELI HILLS

THE ROUTE

It is late in the day – from the top of Foel Drygarn hillfort, the low sun picks out the warm colours of late-flowering heather cut through with green and grey. To the north, the mountains of Eryri (Snowdonia) are a blue smudge across Cardigan Bay, and to the west are Ireland's Wicklow Mountains, faintly visible above the Irish Sea. Balanced on the trig point, arms outstretched, it feels like the whole of Wales is laid out below.

On the North Pembrokeshire Coast, the national park dips inland to include the atmospheric Preseli Hills. They are not particularly tall – Foel Cwmcerwyn is just 536 metres high – but what they lack in elevation they more than make up for with panoramic views and sheer drama: there's a sense of the wild and ancient about these treeless, open hills with their hillforts, wooded valleys, rocky tors and megalithic monuments. Pembrokeshire was renowned for centuries as Gwlad Hud a Lledrith – 'Land of Mystery and Enchantment' – and it is easy to see why as you ride along its most prominent inland ridge.

Stretching from Crymych in the east to the Gwaun Valley to the west, the Golden Road is one of the finest elevated bridleways in Wales. It stays up high for around 11 kilometres, running parallel with a newly discovered Roman road, and is bookended by two dramatic peaks: Foel Eryr ('Place of the Eagle') marks the start of the ridgeline proper, while Foel Drygarn hillfort ('Bare Hill of the Three Cairns') is one of the ridge's most striking landmarks at its eastern end. Just as the name suggests, the hill is topped with three huge, ruined, Bronze Age cairns. These lie within its defensive hilltop enclosure complete with double ramparts and the remains of an Iron Age village containing the foundations of over 200 hut platforms.

High up on Foel Drygarn, the Golden Road can be seen unfurling below. A dark green line cuts through the lighter grassland, following the undulating line of the bare ridge and snaking around a number of mysterious outcrops that sit on the slopes like huge rocky fins. Fractured, angular piles of basalt, dolerite and rhyolite jut out of the landscape, spotted with bristling discs of lichen. The importance of the Golden

NAVIGATION

The bridleway which runs over the top of the Preseli Hills is indistinct in places. If in doubt, stay up on the ridge and aim for the next rocky outcrop. The route follows a waymarked cycle route in Pantmaenog Forest which takes cyclists and horse riders in opposite directions to minimise user conflict. The purpose-built trails around Llys-y-frân Reservoir are well signed and sections can be missed out by staying on the gravel track which circumnavigates the reservoir. At Ty Canol, the route follows a permissive bridleway that is waymarked on the ground but not shown on OS maps.

WHEN TO RIDE

The trails on the Preseli Hills are predominantly grass based and can be boggy in places, even in the driest conditions. It's best to ride here in the spring or summer to reduce damage to the ridgeline trail and maximise enjoyment. The wild flowers here are at their best in late April and early May.

WARNINGS

The main ridge is windswept and exposed with little shelter and few bail-out options.

L–R: *Singletrack on the Golden Road* © Will Kingston-Budge; *Sustrans Route 82 between Felindre Farchog and Nevern; Dyffryn Arms, Cwm Gwaun* © RK; *Pentre Ifan* © RK; *rock formations on the Preseli Hills.*

WATER
Best to carry what you need or fill up at one of the pubs or cafes on the route.

FOOD AND DRINK
- Lakeside Cafe, Llys-y-frân.
T: 01437 532 273
- Tafarn Sinc, Rosebush.
T: 01437 532 214
- The Salutation Inn, Felindre Farchog.
T: 01239 820 564
- Trewern Arms, Nevern.
T: 01239 820 395
- PWNC Cafe, Newport. T: 01239 820 100
- Penlan Uchaf Gardens & Tea Room, Gwaun Valley. T: 01348 881 388
- Dyffryn Arms (Bessie's), Pontfaen (cash and pints of Bass only).
- Globe Inn, Maenclochog.
T: 01437 532 269

Road is still disputed, but it may have once been used to transport gold mined in Ireland's Wicklow Mountains as far as Wessex in South East England. It isn't hard to imagine the trail as a prehistoric trading superhighway though. It would have been an attractive alternative for traders looking to stay clear of the waterlogged lower land – although the elevated bridleway itself gets quite wet and boggy in places even in the height of summer.

While the Golden Road is the centrepiece of the route, the northern slopes of the Preseli Hills have their fair share of quality riding too. The trail drops off the ridge under Foel Drygarn hillfort, first on a stone track and then on a grassy trail which soon becomes little more than a sheep track across the hillside. Dodging gorse bushes and large tufts of grass, it's a fabulous piece of skinny singletrack that keeps you on your toes all the way to the farmhouse near Ty'r-bwich. Further west, after a prolonged stretch on quiet roads, the route descends again through the secretive woods of Ty Canol National Nature Reserve. Dappled singletrack weaves between ancient oak, ash and birch trees, their trunks and branches heaped under so much bright green moss that they are almost indistinguishable from the surrounding moss-covered rocks. In springtime, the woodland floor here is carpeted with bluebells and the tiny white stars of wood anemones.

Ty Canol is part of the largest block of ancient woodland in West Wales and is also home to the famous Neolithic burial site of Pentre Ifan – the first monument in Wales to be given protection under the Ancient Monuments Protection Act in 1884. It is well worth the small detour to see this enormous megalithic structure; it predates Egypt's pyramids, having stood for over 5,000 years. Its large burial mound has long

L–R: Bedd Arthur stone circle; bridleway sign on Bwlch y Pennant.

since gone, exposing six upright stones that are so high that Welsh antiquarian George Owen once wrote that 'a man on horseback may well ride under it without stopping'. Three of the upright stones support a massive, horizontal capstone more than two metres off the ground. It looks precarious but also somehow weightless, as if delicately balanced on upturned fingers.

Below Pentre Ifan, the Nevern Valley has its own secrets. The area is guarded by Mynydd Carningli ('Mountain of Angels') and contains the ruins of Nevern Castle and the Pilgrims' Cross; this rock carving is thought to be part of an old pilgrimage route to St Davids. Down in the valley, Sustrans Route 82 follows an existing bridleway along the Afon Nyfer between Felindre Farchog and Nevern (Nanhyfer) and it is an unexpected delight. The narrow path stays close to the river all the way to St Brynach's Church and is lined with thick banks of wild flowers in spring. Walk up through the avenue of ancient yews (including the famous 'bleeding yew' with its sticky, blood-red sap) to see the huge 10th-century Celtic cross just outside the entrance to the church, as well as the even older Vitalianus Stone nearby.

Once past Newport (Trefdraeth) the route enters the steep-sided Gwaun Valley – yet another secretive woodland world. Here, the inhabitants of Pontfaen and Llanychaer uphold a unique tradition, celebrating New Year's Day – Hen Galan – on 13 January according to the old Julian calendar, which was abolished back in 1752 and replaced with the Gregorian calendar. No trip to the Gwaun Valley is complete, though, without a visit to the Dyffryn Arms, fondly known by locals as 'Bessie's'. This legendary front room pub has been in the same family since 1840. There is no bar as such; drinks are served from a hatch in the tiny front room. There are no pumps either – pints of pale gold Bass are served from a glass jug and drunk on wooden benches surrounded by traditional wallpaper, framed notes and a cosy fireplace.

The final section of the route climbs back over the Preseli Hills to Rosebush, home to a great flooded quarry for swimming and yet another fantastic pub. Tafarn Sinc is instantly recognisable with its bright red corrugated iron cladding, although its rustic interior is just as memorable. Treat yourself to a drink and a home-cooked meal surrounded by agricultural implements lashed to the walls, cured meats dangling from the ceiling and a sawdust-strewn floor. It first opened as the Precelly Hotel in 1876 to serve railway passengers, and was recently saved from closure by an enthusiastic local campaign. Tafarn Sinc now operates as a community-owned pub.

ACCOMMODATION

- Coedfryn Farm Camping, Felindre. T: 07496 283 505
- Wenallt Farm Campsite, Felindre Farchog. T: 01239 820 373
- Ty Canol Farm Campsite, Newport. T: 01239 820 264
- Top of the Woods, Boncath. T: 01239 842 208

Camping pitches will most likely need to be booked well in advance in the summer, as well as during school holidays and bank holidays.

OTHER ROUTES NEARBY

There are more mountain biking trails around the western side of Llys-y-frân Reservoir but they are significantly more technical than the green- and blue-graded trails on the eastern side. Alternatively, start the route from Fishguard and follow Sustrans Route 47 alongside the Gwaun Valley up to Pontfaen. It is a hilly eight kilometres on the road, but the tarmac finishes soon after you reach the wonderful Dyffryn Arms.

BIKE SHOPS AND HIRE

- Llys-y-Frân Lake Bike Hub & Repair Shop. T: 01437 532 273

NOTES

The bike hub at Llys-y-frân (in the outdoor activity centre) has changing rooms, lockers, showers, a bike wash station and bike tools.

04 SARN HELEN & THE GAP ROAD

INTRODUCTION

Bannau Brycheiniog National Park (formerly Brecon Beacons National Park) lies between rural Mid Wales and the southern Valleys. Designated in 1957, its Welsh name translates as 'The Peaks of Brychan's Kingdom'. The area is made up of four ranges: confusingly there is both the Black Mountain in the far west and the Black Mountains to the east, as well as Fforest Fawr and the central Beacons, home to the highest point in southern Britain. Standing at 886 metres, Pen y Fan and its neighbouring peaks have steep north-facing escarpments, great bowl-shaped corries and distinctive, instantly recognisable tabletop summits. The national park is not only an International Dark Sky Reserve; it also contains some of the best-preserved sections of Sarn Helen, the ancient Roman road that once ran the length of Wales. It is also famous for its Waterfall Country, an area with deep wooded gorges, old mining ruins and a staggering number of waterfalls to explore.

ROUTE OVERVIEW

This bikepacking route offers riders a challenging alternative to the Gap Road, a classic mountain biking route in the Bannau with an almost legendary status. Rightly so, as it takes riders high into the central mountains and over the atmospheric Bwlch ar y Fan – the Gap in the Peaks – between Cribyn and Fan y Big. Starting in Neath (Castell-Nedd), the route approaches the Bannau from the coast and links up with the improved Skyline Trail at Afan Forest Park as well as the new flow trails at Dare Valley Gravity Family Bike Park on its way towards Merthyr Tydfil (Merthyr Tudful). Once over the Gap, the route skirts under the national park's steep northern

Previous page: Cribyn seen from Pen y Fan © RK (route 04).

Passing through the Gap (Bwlch ar y Fan) © RK.

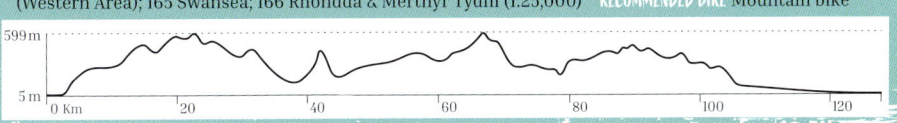

GRADE ▲ **DISTANCE** 127.8km/79.4 miles **ASCENT** 2,170m/7,120ft **TERRAIN** 85% off-road – mainly rough, rocky bridleways **START/FINISH** Neath railway station **START/FINISH GRID REFERENCE** SS 750974 **BIKE-FRIENDLY PUBLIC TRANSPORT** At the start/finish **SATNAV** SA11 1BY **MAP** OS Explorer OL12, Brecon Beacons National Park (Western Area); 165 Swansea; 166 Rhondda & Merthyr Tydfil (1:25,000) **RECOMMENDED BIKE** Mountain bike

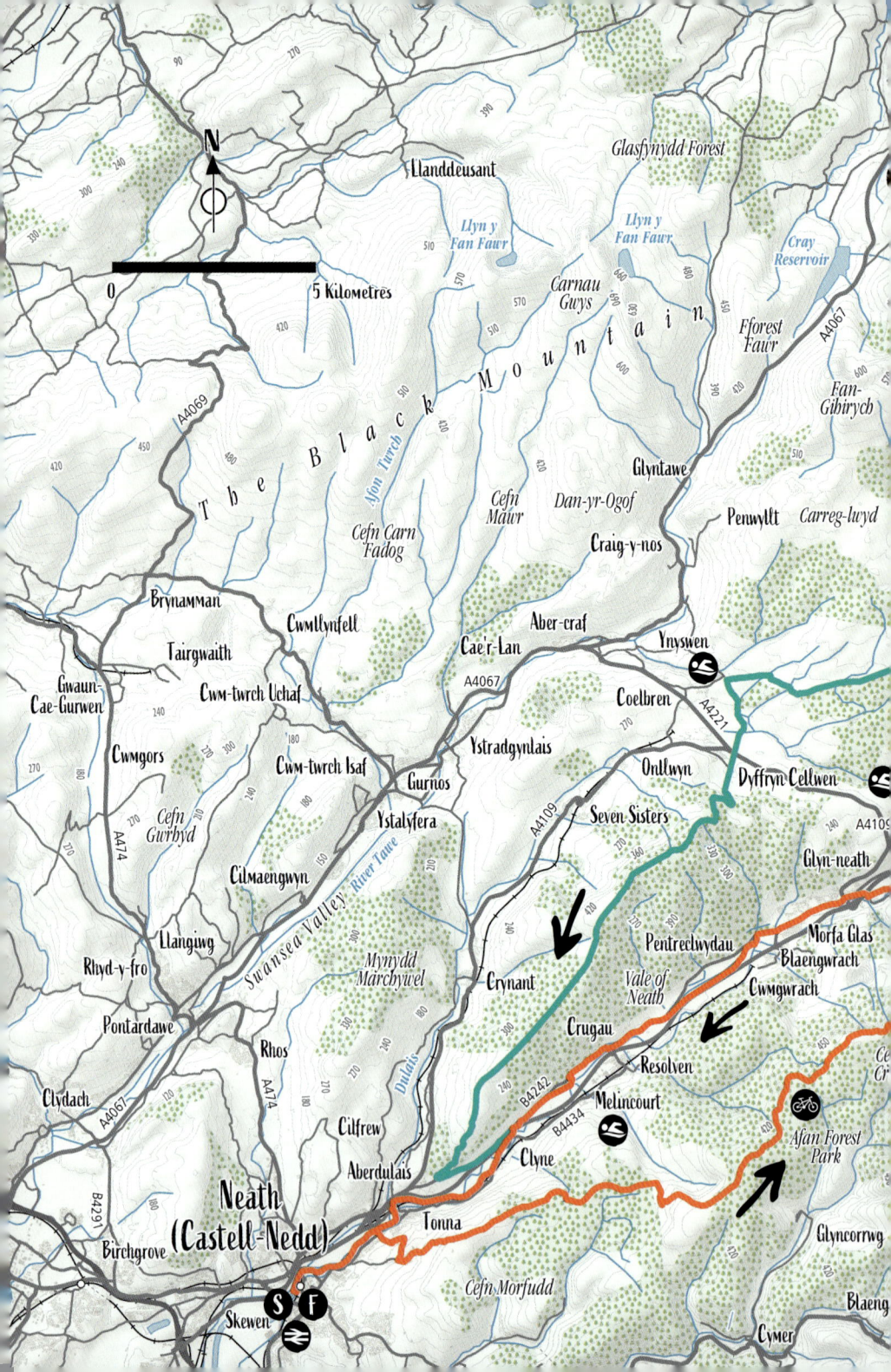

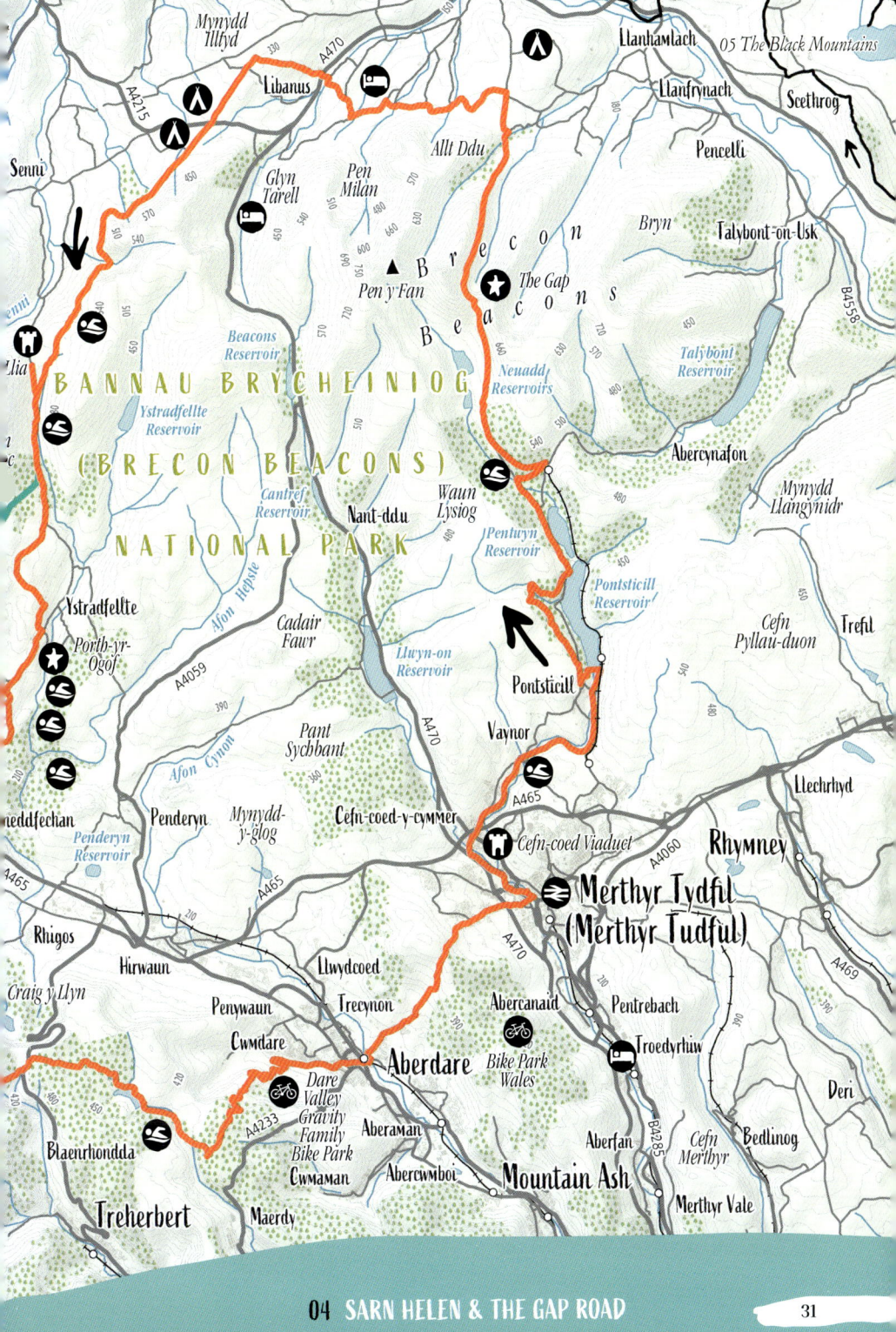

slopes before following Sarn Helen south across Fforest Fawr with its impressive waterfalls, limestone pavements, caves and standing stones. There is wonderfully little tarmac, but be prepared for some significant elevation and extremely rough and rocky trails.

THE ROUTE

Turning off the forest track and leaving the shelter of the trees, the trail emerges out on to the edge of a sheer escarpment. Like the Bannau in miniature, two grassy natural amphitheatres curve away to the east, scooped and hollowed by ice. A piece of narrow singletrack cuts across the steep slopes ahead, picking its way through rocks and skirting high above the dark waters of Llyn Fawr and Llyn Fach. In the distance, the distinctive flat-topped summits of the central Beacons appear tantalisingly close – daring, goading and coaxing you on in equal measure.

For riders looking for a bikepacking challenge to rival the Gap Road, this route is a satisfying way to approach the central Beacons, and just as testing. Rather than beginning in the mountains, this route makes its way inland from the industrial south coast, working its way up and over the Valleys to reach the edge of Bannau Brycheiniog (Brecon Beacons) National Park. The distinctive flat-topped summits of Pen y Fan and Corn Du are constants in a rapidly changing landscape of wind turbines, open hillside and forestry plantations, their angular profiles an ever-present feature on the skyline to the north. Even when hidden from view, they linger on the periphery: a possible sighting through a break in the trees, a silhouette glimpsed out of the corner of an eye. Out of sight but never out of mind.

Leaving the Vale of Neath, the route draws together a combination of natural and man-made trails on its way towards the national park boundary. Afan may not have been the first mountain biking trail centre in Wales, but it has helped pioneer trail design and construction over the years, with trail builders Russ Burton, Hugh Clixby and Rowan Sorrell all involved in its evolution. Above the centre at Glyncorrwg, the route joins the

NAVIGATION

The bridleway under the Ivy Tower above Tonna has been diverted round Dan-y-lan Farm. The route joins a number of clearly waymarked Sustrans routes, including the high-level route 47 (the Celtic Trail) out of Neath, route 8 (the Taff Trail) between Merthyr Tydfil and Taf Fechan, and route 46 back into Neath along the canal. Look out for the Skyline Trail's striking yellow and black signs at Afan – they show a mountain biker riding against a backdrop of two stars and a crescent moon. At Pontsticill Reservoir, the route follows the helpful 'Brecon Beacons mountain bike route' signs (a green arrow inside a black and white circle) all the way over the Gap.

WHEN TO RIDE

The trail surfaces in the central Beacons are predominantly stone based and hold up well all year. However, the Gap Road climbs up over the bwlch (pass) between Cribyn and Fan y Big on high, mountainous terrain and is a serious undertaking regardless of the weather or season. In the summer months, the waterfalls and plunge pools around Ystradfellte get very busy.

L–R: *Maen Llia standing stone © RK; descending below the north face of Cribyn © RK; tackling the Gap Road's upper section © RK; Sgwd y Pannwr © RK; Craig y Llyn escarpment © RK.*

WARNINGS

This route links up with the red-graded Skyline Trail at Afan as well as the new flow trails in the Dare Valley – both can be avoided if needed. The trail surface of Sarn Helen varies greatly along its length; the section between Heol Senni and Coelbren is known locally as the 'Road to Hell' and is extremely rough and rocky. There are No Camping signs around the reservoirs and Cwm Taf Fechan. There are also two awkward gates on Sustrans Route 47 which you may have to lift your bike over (grid references: SS 835999; SS 850994).

WATER

There are plenty of accessible streams and rivers to fill up from en route. Highlights include the fords across Nant Cwm-du and Nedd Fechan (optional route), and the Nant Ystwyth and Taf Fechan waterfalls.

Skyline Trail which had been closed between 2012 and 2021 due to the construction of the Pen y Cymoedd Wind Farm. A mix of singletrack and gravel roads weave their way through pine trees and wind turbines, the deep hum of their huge blades coming and going in waves.

Often overlooked in favour of the forest's popular Y Wal, White's Level and Blade trails, the Skyline Trail has now been redesigned with three new sections – *Bwa* (Bow), *Saeth* (Arrow) and *Saethwr* (Archer). The old singletrack skirting around the Craig y Llyn escarpment, though, is still the real draw. It is narrow and exposed in places, with sweeping views out to the Bannau in the north and a steep drop to Llyn Fawr and Llyn Fach below. The larger of these two lakes is the site of the famous Llyn Fawr Hoard, where 21 bronze and iron objects were discovered when the lake was deepened into a reservoir in 1909. A spearhead, axe heads, a sword and two enormous cauldrons were all found preserved in the waterlogged peat. The Skyline Trail sections included on the route are rocky, but never that technical, as they undulate along the escarpment edge – they can be easily avoided by staying on Sustrans Route 47 through the forest. Just past Castell Nos Reservoir, the new flow trails at Dare Valley Gravity Family Bike Park (free entry) make for a contrasting smooth roller-coaster descent into Aberdare (Aberdâr).

North of Merthyr Tydfil, the route enters Bannau Brycheiniog National Park, passes a series of reservoirs and joins the classic Gap Road mountain biking loop. Both the 'gap' and the 'road' are visible right from the bottom; a grassy picnic site with a pretty arched bridge, miniature waterfalls and plunge pools marks the start of the climb proper. Soon a wide, rocky track branches off from the road, gaining height steadily across the open moorland. Despite the roughness of the trail surface and a small but steep-sided ravine to negotiate, this gradual southern approach does little to prepare you for the shape and scale of the central Beacons. As you ride through Bwlch ar y Fan – the 'Gap in the Peaks' – the north-facing cliffs drop away dramatically into Cwm Cynwyn below. It is one enormous natural amphitheatre hollowed out from ice – its ridgeline curving and scalloped and its grassy face streaked with dark bands of rock. As the track starts descending, the red earthen walls rise to head height, a series of rock steps come into sight, and the riding becomes all-consuming until you reach a left-hand bend. From here, it is a bumpy and rocky blast down the valley towards Brecon (Aberhonddu).

Once up and over the Gap Road, the route heads west to explore Fforest Fawr UNESCO Global Geopark and some of the most remote and quiet corners of the national park. Tucked above Heol Senni, the steep rock walls of the Craig Cerrig

FOOD AND DRINK
- Black Rock Cafe, Dare Valley Country Park. T: 01594 729 007
- The Aberglais, Vaynor. T: 01685 377 344
- The Red Cow Inn, Pontsticill. T: 01685 387 775
- The Old Barn Tea Rooms, Ystradgynwyn (seasonal). T: 01685 373 175
- The Tai'r Bull Inn, Libanus. T: 01874 622 600
- Caffi Y Fan, Bannau Brycheiniog National Park Visitor Centre, Libanus. T: 01874 623 366
- Meat & Greet Co., Dove Workshop, Banwen. T: 01639 700 633
- Canalside Cafe, South Wales Adventure Company, Resolven (seasonal). T: 07554 306 193

There are plenty of other options in Aberdare and Merthyr Tydfil.

ACCOMMODATION
- The Roost, Merthyr Tydfil. T: 07484 697 392
- Cefn Cantref Campsite, Brecon. T: 01874 622 626
- Penstar Bunkhouse, Libanus. T: 01874 622 702
- Pwllyn Farm Camping, Libanus. T: 01874 636 785
- Brecon Beacons Wild Camping, Lower Forest Lodge Farm, Brecon. T: 07444 896 883
- YHA Brecon Beacons, Libanus. T: 0345 371 9029

L–R: *Restricted byway above Ystradfellte © RK; sunrise over the Bannau © RK.*

CAMPING ON FARMS

Farmers and other landowners in the national park often allow occasional camping on their land for a small charge. Many have few facilities and offer a nearly wild camping experience. It is advised that they are contacted in advance of a stay.

- Neuadd Farm, Cantref.
T: 01874 665 247. Grid reference: SO 042247. Very basic site, water available, booking required for groups.
- Cwmcynwyn Farm, Cantref.
T: 01874 665 378. Grid reference: SO 039235. Water and toilets available.
- Blaen-nedd isaf, Ystradfellte.
T: 01639 721 847. Grid reference: SN 911144. Very basic site, water available, booking required for groups.
- Pentwyn-Einon Farm Bungalow, Ystradfellte. T: 01639 720 542. Grid reference: SN 926132. Water and toilets available.
- The New Inn Pub, Ystradfellte.
T: 01639 721 014. Grid reference: SN 929135. Water and toilets available (in pub).
- Bryn Bwch Farm, Pontneddfechan.
T: 07929 828 667. Grid reference: SN 919116. Water and toilets available.

There is also a designated backpacking site by the ruins of Llech Llia (SN 922193) which is available outside of

L–R: *Bluebells above Nedd Fechan © RK; modern mosaic at Banwen; MTB route signs; Pen y Fan and Corn Du.*

Gleisiad and Fan Frynych National Nature Reserve have a very different feel to the central Beacons. Their shady north-facing crags are covered in hawthorn, rowan and ash that create a sort of vertical woodland amphitheatre, while the rocks shelter rare Arctic–alpine plants like roseroot and purple saxifrage, survivors from the last ice age. This secretive, remote landscape is also crossed by a section of the ancient Roman road known as Sarn Helen. This strategic, north–south highway would have been an important addition to the network of roads built by the Romans as part of their military campaign in Wales, and was named after Saint Elen, an early founder of churches in Wales and wife of the Roman emperor Magnus Maximus. Riding along this lonely stretch of road, it is easy to imagine a Roman legion marching through these mountains. In places, you can still see the cobbled surface laid by its builders: it's tough, rough and rocky, and built to withstand the Welsh weather.

After a recommended optional detour to visit the impressive

Maen Llia standing stone, there is a choice to be made: either follow the optional route and continue on the increasingly rocky Roman road back towards Neath, or stay on the main route, leaving the Roman road to discover the area's famous Waterfall Country. Centred around Ystradfellte, there are deep valleys, wooded gorges, caves, potholes, and an astonishing number of waterfalls and plunge pools to explore including Sgŵd Clun-gwyn ('Fall of the White Meadow'), Sgwd yr Elra ('Fall of Snow') and Sgŵd y Pannwr ('Fall of the Fuller' – an old occupation dating back to Roman times which involved the washing of wool). The riding is just as surprising. A network of bridleways criss-crosses the grassy meadows and limestone pavements, and the route follows one up a lane bounded by high stone walls and wide grassy verges. You could be forgiven for thinking you had been dropped into a little corner of the Yorkshire Dales. The resemblance is uncanny; it looks just like Mastiles Lane.

lambing season (15 April to 10 May). There are no facilities, but there is water from the nearby stream and spring. Approach through the gate just north of the Maen Llia standing stone. Please seek prior permission from the Cnewr Estate manager on 01874 636 448.

OTHER ROUTES NEARBY

Sustrans Route 8 follows the Taff Trail south all the way to Cardiff, which is also the final section of the Lôn Las Cymru long-distance cycling route.

BIKE SHOPS AND HIRE

- Afan Valley Bike Shed, Afan Forest Park.
  T: 01639 850 800
- Dare Valley Gravity Family Bike Park Workshop and Bike Shop, Aberdare.
  T: 01685 874672
- VS-Cycles, Merthyr Tydfil.
  T: 07854 949 148
- Bikes and Hikes, Talybont-on-Usk.
  T: 07909 968 135

NOTES

Bannau Brycheiniog is pronounced 'ban-aye bruch-ay-nee-og'. It contains a non-English sound represented by the 'ch', as in the Scottish loch.

SUPPORT

The Afan Trail Volunteers group is responsible for helping to maintain the mountain bike trails in the Afan Valley: www.afantrailvolunteers.co.uk

05 THE BLACK MOUNTAINS

INTRODUCTION
The Black Mountains form a triangle of grassy, rolling uplands between the towns of Abergavenny (Y Fenni), Brecon (Aberhonddu) and Hay-on-Wye (Y Gelli Gandryll). Extending east across the border into Herefordshire and separated from the central Beacons by the River Usk, it is unsurprising that they look and feel a little different to the rest of Bannau Brycheiniog (Brecon Beacons) National Park. There's still the same distinctive red sandstone bedrock, those long, lung-bursting climbs and that remote high mountain feeling, but gone are the sharp ridges, huge reservoirs and dramatic waterfalls. Instead, you'll find long grassy ridges and narrow valleys, hillsides of bracken grazed by Welsh mountain ponies and the small but perfectly formed peaks of Sugar Loaf (Y Fâl) and Skirrid Fawr (Ysgyryd Fawr).

ROUTE OVERVIEW
This strenuous route starts in the picturesque market town of Brecon and makes its way east on the Monmouthshire and Brecon Canal before reaching the Black Mountains proper. It is a deceptively long, flat warm-up on tarmac. Riding here usually requires a substantial amount of climbing, and this route is no exception. On the way, it crosses multiple valleys and tackles the steep, northern escarpment above Talgarth with some inevitable hike-a-bike, but the rewards are some exceptional trails that hold their own against the best in the UK. There's the Mynydd Llangorse singletrack – a delightful contouring sliver of red earth, the never-ending descent off Cefn Moel to Bwlch, and the drop off Crug Mawr with its wild combination of heather-lined singletrack, open ridgeline riding and a rocky final plummet to reach the river.

Descent off Crug Mawr © RK.

GRADE ▲ **DISTANCE** 96.6km/60 miles **ASCENT** 2,200m/7,218ft **TERRAIN** 80% off-road, with a mix of forestry tracks, grassy bridleways and singletrack; some challenging climbs and rocky descents **START/FINISH** Brecon **START/FINISH GRID REFERENCE** SO 043286 **BIKE-FRIENDLY PUBLIC TRANSPORT** Nearest station is Abergavenny, 15km off-route from Llanbedr **SATNAV** LD3 9AL **MAP** OS Explorer OL12, Brecon Beacons National Park (Western Area); OL13, Brecon Beacons National Park (Eastern Area) (1:25,000) **RECOMMENDED BIKE** Mountain bike

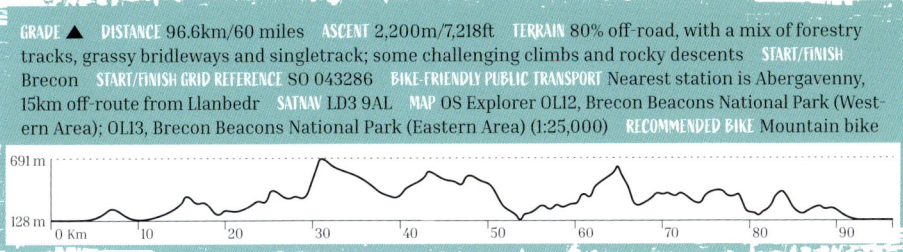

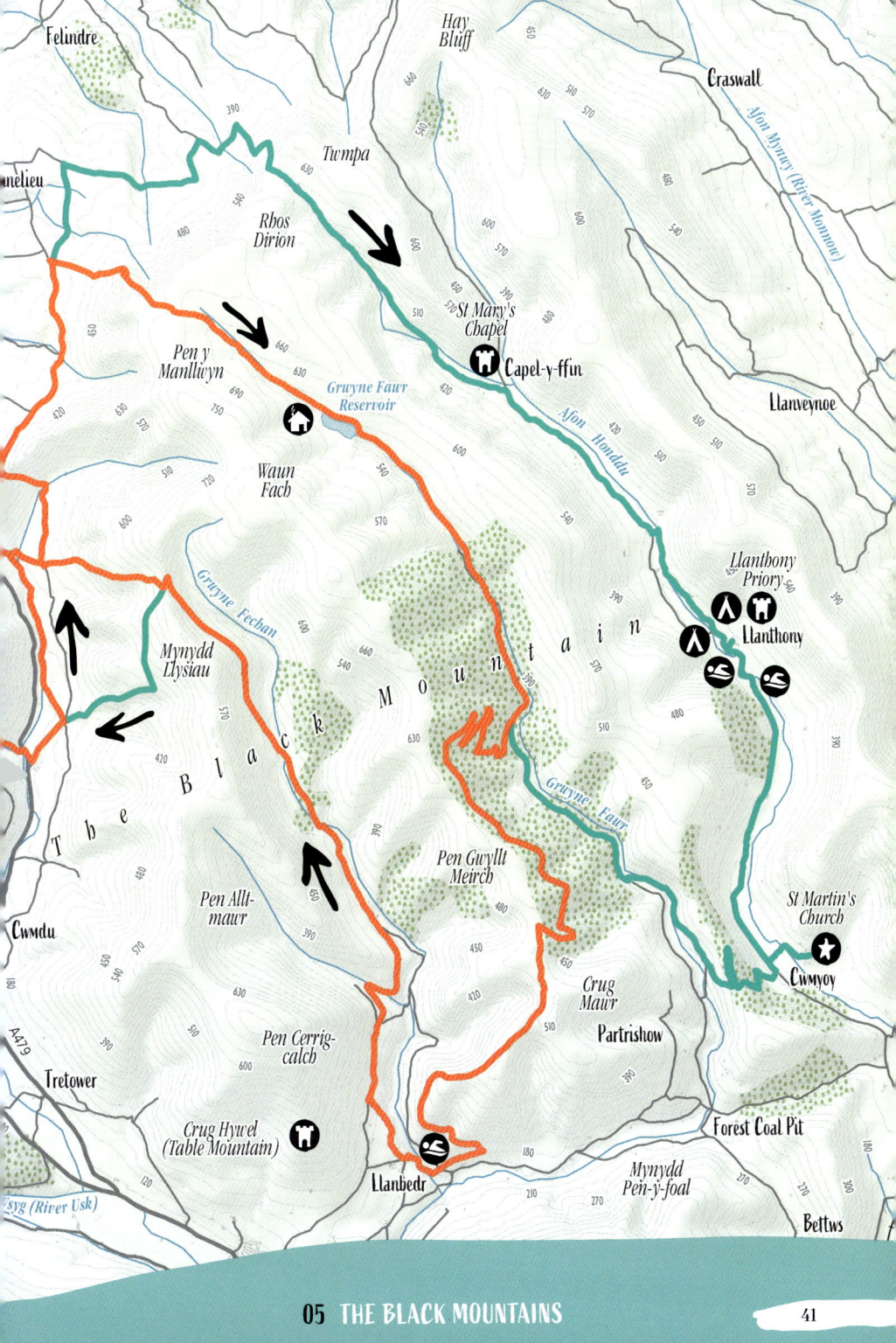

THE ROUTE

'To the west ... ran the Black Mountains: mile after mile of bracken and whin and heather, of black marsh and green springy turf, of rowan and stunted thorn and myrtle and bog-cotton, roamed by the mountain sheep and the wild ponies ... Fields climbed unevenly into the mountains, and far up on the black ridges stood isolated white farmhouses and grey barns.' Raymond Williams, *Border Country* (1960)

Growing up in the village of Pandy right on the edge of the Black Mountains, Raymond Williams knew this corner of Bannau Brycheiniog (Brecon Beacons) like the back of his hand. These mountains straddle the border between England and Wales, stretching east into Herefordshire. Yet, despite being within touching distance of Abergavenny, it is remarkable how isolated and profoundly peaceful they feel. Narrow lanes wind their way up the long valleys past lonely chapels, farms and old ruins, while the thin, whaleback ridges are usually empty save for mountain sheep, wild ponies and the odd cyclist.

In his book *People of the Black Mountains* (1989), Williams begins by inviting readers unfamiliar with the area to create their own 'hand of the Black Mountains' – a sort of portable, topographical map of its ridges, valleys and rivers rendered out of muscle and bone:

'See this layered sandstone in the short mountain grass. Place your right hand on it, palm downward. See where the summer sun rises and where it stands at noon. Direct your index finger midway between them. Spread your fingers, not widely. You now hold this place in your hand.'

It is an image that feels laden with responsibility, but also possibility. Considering the compact nature of the Black Mountains, a quick glance at an OS map reveals a surprisingly large network of bridleways. They criss-cross the mountain's slender, finger-like ridges and very rarely stay up high for long.

Riding east out of Brecon and along the Monmouthshire and Brecon Canal, the whaleback ridges of the Black Mountains look small and unassuming in the distance. Llangors Lake (Llyn Syfaddan) – the largest natural lake in South Wales – is worth a short detour to see its famous crannog at the Welsh

NAVIGATION

The maze of forestry tracks in Mynydd Du Forest can be confusing – follow the helpful Brecon Beacons mountain bike route signs (a green arrow inside a black and white circle) all the way up to the ridgeline at the edge of the forest.

WHEN TO RIDE

The singletrack here comes into its own in the spring and early summer. It holds up fairly well into autumn, although the bridleway around the bulk of Mynydd Troed can get extremely muddy after wet weather. In the summer, some of the bridleways become very overgrown due to narrow hedgerows particularly around Allt yr Esgair hillfort, and the rapid growth of bracken can reach head height in places, especially on the descent off Cockit Hill to the hamlet of Waun Fach.

WARNINGS

The route climbs up over two exposed mountain passes *(bylchau)*; each pass is over 600 metres which is higher than the Gap Road (see route 04, page 29). Rhiw Trumau is one of the route's roughest bridleways – for a smoother descent, take the grassy bridleway that leads south from the col under Pen Trumau instead. Access to Grwyne Fawr bothy is down a steep bank and it is best to carry a back-up shelter as the building is tiny.

L–R: *The Welsh Crannog Centre, Llangors Lake; signing the bothy book* © RK; *Table Mountain (Crug Hywel)* © RK; *Llanthony Priory* © RK; *Grwyne Fawr bothy.*

WATER
The more remote eastern section of the route passes lots of accessible rivers, including Grwyne Fechan, Grwyne Fawr and Afon Honddu.

FOOD AND DRINK
- Lake Cafe, Llangorse (seasonal).
  T: 07583 988 730
- Llanthony Treats, Llanthony.
  T: 01873 890 867
- Llanthony Priory Hotel and Cellar Bar, Llanthony. T: 01873 890 487
- Half Moon Inn, Llanthony.
  T: 01873 890 611
- The Red Lion, Llanbedr.
  T: 01873 810 754
- Dinas Castle Inn, Pengenffordd.
  T: 01874 711 353
- New Inn & Beacons Backpackers, Bwlch. T: 01874 730 215
- Beacons Farm Shop, Welsh Venison Centre, Bwlch. T: 01874 730 929

ACCOMMODATION
- Grwyne Fawr Bothy (Mountain Bothies Association) –
  www.mountainbothies.org.uk
- Llanthony Treats Camping and Bunkhouse, Llanthony.
  T: 01873 890 867
- Llanthony Court Bunk Barn and Camping, Llanthony. T: 01873 890 359
- Dinas Castle Inn Bunkhouse, Pengenffordd. T: 01874 711 353
- Gilfach Camping, Llangorse.
  T: 01874 658 272
- New Inn & Beacons Backpackers, Bwlch. T: 01874 730 215
- The Star Bunkhouse, Bwlch.
  T: 01874 730 080

Crannog Centre (free entry). This ancient artificial island was constructed out on the water and is thought to have been built as the royal seat of Brycheiniog, an early medieval Welsh kingdom that ruled over the area in the ninth century. Crannogs have been found all over Scotland and Ireland, but the Llangors crannog is unique: it is the only one that has ever been found in Wales.

Past Llangors Lake, the route heads into the mountains. Up on Cockit Hill, the singletrack road climbs steeply to the pass between the peaks of Mynydd Llangorse and Mynydd Troed, and it is hard not to be struck by their 'extraordinary richness of colour, too brilliant really to be credible at first', as Williams writes in *Border Country*. In the summer sun, the grass on the Black Mountains turns a rich olive green and the slopes are crossed with deep, red earth tracks known locally as 'rhiws'. It's harder still not to marvel at the Mynydd Llangorse bridleway which starts at the road pass here – in the summer, the colourful, loamy soil cuts a narrow singletrack through the bracken as it contours round the mountain slopes. Autumn can be just as memorable though. The singletrack won't be at its dusty-dry best, but it becomes sweet with the smell of fallen crab apples and whole swathes of hillside are transformed under rich russet-coloured bracken.

The route climbs on a stony track up to the ruins of Castell Dinas – the highest castle in Wales – and over the shapely ridge known as the Dragon's Back, before making its way round to the northern slopes of the Black Mountains. They have a very different feel to the rest of the area; the long parallel ridges come together in a high mountain plateau and steep escarpment, creating an imposing wall above Talgarth. There are three possible choices once you get there: a byway which

climbs up and over to Grwyne Fawr Reservoir and its tiny mountain bothy (shown on the map as the main route); a bridleway which zigzags up Rhiw Wen in the shadow of Twmpa (also known as Lord Hereford's Knob and shown on the map as an alternative route); and a final option to join the Gospel Pass – the highest road pass in Wales. Whichever option you pick, they all involve some inevitable hike-a-bike.

The latter two route options both end up in the Vale of Ewyas. Named after the small Welsh kingdom of Ewias which was established after the Romans left Wales in the fifth century, the valley is home to the atmospheric ruins of Llanthony Priory (free entry). The priory's huge, elegant arches are well worth exploring, as well as the pub/cafe which is tucked away in one of the ruin's 13th-century vaulted cellars, hidden down a flight of stairs. The valley itself feels cut off from the outside world despite the quiet lane that works its way up to the pass. Its narrow size adds to the feeling of being completely encircled by mountains. The valley only starts to open out as you reach the charming St Martin's Church and its crooked tower.

Working its way back west, the route saves two of the biggest climbs until last, but also two of the best descents. Crug Mawr is wonderfully long and drawn out, hugging the edge of Mynydd Du Forest before following the Beacons Way along the open ridgeline. Up on the heather slopes, the trail points straight across the valley to the flat top of Table Mountain, and soon the conical peak of the Sugar Loaf comes into view too. Dark, peaty singletrack gives way to smooth grass, steepening as it approaches the trees, and then a gate leads to a final rocky section down to the river. Rhiw Trumau is a little shorter, launching off the grassy col to race across the hillside below Waun Fach before an even rockier descent to reach the road.

CAMPING ON FARMS

Farmers and other landowners in the national park often allow occasional camping on their land for a small charge. Many have few facilities and offer a nearly wild camping experience. It is advised that they are contacted in advance of a stay.

- Ty-Mawr, Llanbedr. T: 01873 810 606. Grid reference: SO 235206. Water and toilets available.
- Gudder Farm, Llanbedr. T: 01873 810 472. Grid reference: SO 245203. Very basic site, water available.

OTHER ROUTES NEARBY

Start at Abergavenny railway station instead and join the route north of Crickhowell – the larger eastern loop will give a nice sample of the riding on the Black Mountains, and it still has some good overnight options.

BIKE SHOPS AND HIRE

- Bikes and Hikes, Talybont-on-Usk. T: 07909 968 135
- Biped Cycles, Brecon. T: 01874 622 296
- Black Mountains Cycleworks, Forest Coalpit. T: 07946 356 439
- Drover Cycles, Hay-on-Wye. T: 01497 822 419

The Talybont Bike Hub in Talybont-on-Usk is another good base to use (SO 112228, LD3 7YQ). There is free parking at the hub in the village hall car park (donations welcome), as well as public toilets, showers and a bike washing area (bring change).

L–R: *Descending from Grwyne Fawr Reservoir dam © RK; sunrise over the Black Mountains © RK.*

06 CARDIFF & THE VALLEYS

INTRODUCTION
Sitting at the mouth of the River Taff on the Severn Estuary, Cardiff (Caerdydd) was once the capital of the world's coal trade. At its height, a fifth of the world's fuel passed through its docks. Fast forward a century and the coal is long gone, but Cardiff is now both the Welsh capital and one of the most popular tourist destinations in Wales, featuring Cardiff Castle, Bute Park, the world-famous Principality Stadium and the Senedd – the home of the Welsh Parliament. Nearby, too, is fairy-tale Castell Coch, and Caerphilly Castle – the largest castle in Wales with its very own leaning tower, even wonkier than Pisa's. The surrounding windswept uplands and deep-wooded vales known locally as 'the Valleys' provide a stark contrast to the city; despite the wind turbines and occasional motocross ruts, the hills here feel gloriously wild and unexpectedly remote.

ROUTE OVERVIEW
This fairly mellow, gravel-bike-friendly route is ideal for riders looking for an accessible overnight adventure. Starting right in the heart of Cardiff city centre, the route follows the Taff Trail north out of the city to explore the bridleways that cross the grassy ridgeways high above Caerphilly and the Rhymney Valley. The riding is wonderfully varied and surprisingly tranquil so close to the capital; there's narrow, fast-rolling singletrack over Rudry Common, a fantastic series of beech-lined bridleways between Machen and Castell Coch, easy cruising on tarmac cycle paths and some stiff climbs to reach the exposed, open tracks across the commons. The route goes past Parc Penallta – home to a huge earthen sculpture known as Sultan the Pit Pony, Cwmcarn's purpose-built trails

Singletrack on Mynydd Rudry.

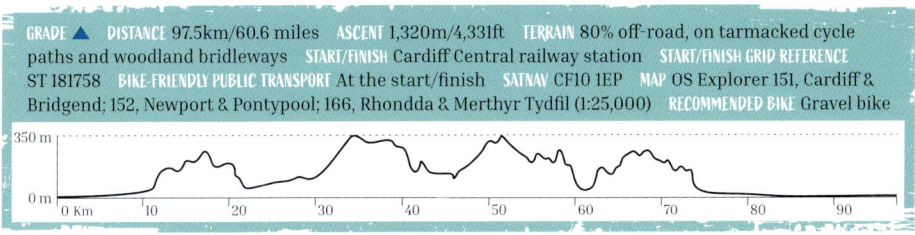

GRADE ▲ DISTANCE 97.5km/60.6 miles ASCENT 1,320m/4,331ft TERRAIN 80% off-road, on tarmacked cycle paths and woodland bridleways START/FINISH Cardiff Central railway station START/FINISH GRID REFERENCE ST 181758 BIKE-FRIENDLY PUBLIC TRANSPORT At the start/finish SATNAV CF10 1EP MAP OS Explorer 151, Cardiff & Bridgend; 152, Newport & Pontypool; 166, Rhondda & Merthyr Tydfil (1:25,000) RECOMMENDED BIKE Gravel bike

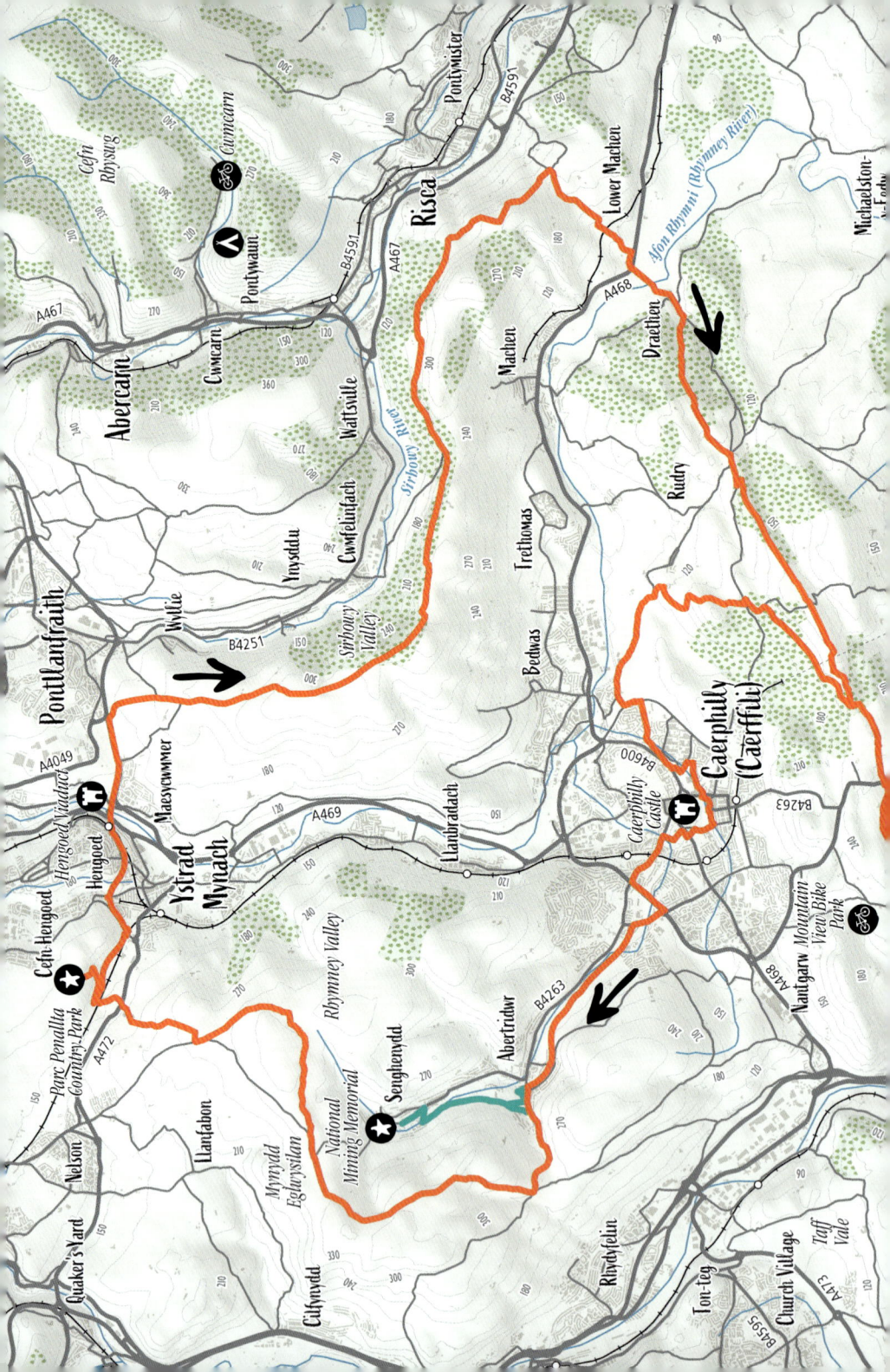

BIKEPACKING WALES

are temptingly close by, and there is a recommended loop exploring scenic Cardiff Bay and the barrage, which can be ridden either at the start or end of the ride.

THE ROUTE

Emerging out of dappled beech woods, the bridleway comes to an abrupt end. On the map, its green dashed line marches blithely on, ploughing straight over the quarry lip, down its sheer cliffs and across the flat, grassy quarry floor the size of a football pitch. Seen from above, the ghostly path picks its way through rusting industrial relics, around the scars of old campfires and past a collection of stones that have been rearranged to spell out the names of strangers.

Much like the bridleway through the disused quarry above Caerphilly (Caerffili), this route is full of startling and unexpected sights for such a compact urban adventure. It sets off from Cardiff Central railway station, quickly leaving the bustle and noise of the capital behind on the Taff Trail. The largely traffic-free, tarmacked trail follows an abandoned branch of the Taff Vale Railway and parts of the old Glamorganshire Canal that were once used to transport coal and iron ore from Merthyr Tydfil (Merthyr Tudful) and the surrounding area to the docks at Cardiff. It's a remarkable natural corridor along the river; it cuts a peaceful swathe right through the city and is home to wildlife including herons, cormorants, kingfishers and even otters.

The Taff Trail also passes through Bute Park – one of the largest urban parks in Europe. Formerly owned by the Bute family, the Fifth Marquess of Bute gifted the extensive grounds to the people of Cardiff in 1947. The entrance on Castle Street goes through a crenelated gatehouse which is part of the famous Animal Wall – look out for a huge, stone-carved hyena, wolf, beaver, lion, anteater and a wonderfully haughty-looking pelican looking down its beak at people on the pavement below. The park also conceals 2,000 years of history; Cardiff Castle's (£) huge walls are completely obscured by the park's mature trees in the summer until you are almost underneath them.

Further north, there is another surprise as you emerge from

NAVIGATION NOTES

The start and finish of the route follow the waymarked Taff Trail (Sustrans Route 8) between Cardiff and Castell Coch. The route also intermittently follows the Rhymney Valley Ridgeway Walk.

WHEN TO RIDE

The off-road sections get quite muddy in the winter months, especially the bridleways and byways on the exposed commons and the wooded section along the Rhymney Valley Ridgeway Walk. However, much of the route is on well-surfaced cycleways.

WARNINGS

The route skirts the edge of Castell Heights Golf Club. Follow the route carefully around the disused quarry at Cefn Onn (ST 173851) – the bridleway marked on OS maps plunges over the cliffs. Bute Park opens at 7.30 a.m. and closes 30 minutes before sunset. Daily closing times are displayed on site.

L–R: *Bridleway on the Rhymney Valley Ridgeway; Wales Millennium Centre © RK; Caerphilly Castle © RK; the Pierhead Building at night © RK; coal miner sculpture, Cardiff Bay © RK.*

WATER

There are many pubs, cafes and shops to fill up from on the route.

FOOD AND DRINK

- The Travellers Rest, Thornhill.
  T: 02920 859 021
- The Old Library, Caerphilly.
  T: 02920 885 243
- The Castle Inn, Cwmcarn Forest Drive.
  T: 01495 272 877
- Crosskeys Fish Bar, Crosskeys.
  T: 01495 270 420
- Maenllwyd Inn, Rudry.
  T: 02920 882 372

There are plenty of amenities in Cardiff and the surrounding towns and villages, such as Hengoed, Pentlwyn, Crosskeys and Caerphilly.

ACCOMMODATION

- Cwmcarn Forest Campsite, Newport.
  T: 01495 272 001

a concrete underpass below the A470. Straight ahead, Castell Coch's fairy-tale towers peek out of the ancient beech woods of Fforest-fawr, their conical roofs unmistakable even from this distance. The 'Red Castle' (£) was built in the 19th century for the absurdly wealthy Third Marquess of Bute. It is a magnificent medieval fantasy castle complete with a vaulted great hall, octagonal drawing room, a drawbridge and portcullis, and a timber fighting gallery. Look underneath all the mock-medieval splendour though and you can see the remains of the 13th-century fortress belonging to the ruthless Marcher Lord, Gilbert de Clare, who also built Caerphilly Castle (£) nearby. Up on the bare hills of Mynydd Eglwysilan common, the faint remains of the Senghenydd Dyke are still visible too, marking the boundary of his once-extensive hunting grounds.

Past Castell Coch, the route follows a long, wooded ridgeline high above the Rhymney Valley. In Fforest-fawr, the smooth gravel forest tracks pass by a series of intricately carved wooden sculptures of wizards, dragons and woodland animals, while on Cefncarnau-fach the bridleway narrows to singletrack around the edge of a golf course. The trail climbs and descends through a forest of beech trees, lined either side with high grassy banks and thick, gnarled trunks. Every now and then it breaks out of the trees, emerging on to open hillside. From here, the long, thin Welsh Valleys and their iconic rows of terraced houses are hidden from sight. Instead, the hills look like one large, rolling plateau stretching north towards Bannau Brycheiniog – a serene illusion broken only by the occasional muffled blast of a train horn from the valleys below.

While the hills are largely peaceful now, they would have been a hive of industry in the 19th and 20th centuries as Wales

became the first industrial nation of the world. The route passes through a number of former coal mining communities, and they have each remembered the legacy of the area's heritage in unique and touching ways. In the Aber Valley, the route goes past the site of the Universal Colliery which suffered the most lethal mining explosion in British history in 1913. Now the former mining community is home to Wales's first national mining monument – the Senghenydd National Mining Memorial. It can be visited by following Sustrans Route 475 into the village. The nearby Parc Penallta country park (free entry) has been built on reclaimed land which was originally the Penallta Colliery before it closed in 1991. It found an imaginative use for the mine's huge spoil heaps, commissioning Welsh landscape sculptor Mick Petts to carve out an enormous galloping horse – known as 'Sultan the Pit Pony' – from the waste material. The grass sculpture is 200 metres long and 15 metres high, and a lasting tribute to the men, women, children and animals that toiled in the dark to help pull millions of tons of black gold out of the earth.

Retracing its steps, the route heads back into Cardiff's city centre where a recommended loop takes riders on a tour of the newly regenerated and vibrant waterfront of Cardiff Bay. The 10-kilometre Cardiff Bay Trail takes in many of the historic buildings that were once part of the flourishing coal industry here, like the old Custom House, the Norwegian Church, the D-Shed and the Coal Exchange – famous for being the place where the world's first £1 million cheque was signed. Cycling over the Cardiff Bay Barrage is a real highlight, surrounded on one side by an enormous freshwater lake and on the other by the choppy waters of the Severn Estuary.

OTHER ROUTES NEARBY

The route briefly joins the Celtic Trail (Sustrans Route 47), a long-distance trail that stretches across the entire breadth of South Wales, from the Irish Sea to the English border. The Ely Trail links Cardiff Bay to St Fagans National Museum of History on an 11-kilometre, mostly traffic-free path.

BIKE SHOPS AND HIRE

- Tom's Cycle Shed, Tongwynlais.
  T: 07769 687 606
- Cardiff Cycle Workshop, Cardiff.
  T: 02920 616 783
- Ps Cycles, Cwmcarn Forest Drive.
  T: 01495 272 279

NOTES

The Bike Lock (£) in Cardiff city centre provides secure bike storage during the day, as well as e-bike charging points, a shower, lockers and changing facilities.

L–R: *The Pierhead Building, Cardiff Bay © RK; Castell Coch; byway above Senghenydd © RK.*

07 LOWER WYE VALLEY & THE FOREST OF DEAN

INTRODUCTION
The lower stretches of the River Wye (Afon Gwy) pass through the Wye Valley Area of Outstanding Natural Beauty (AONB) – famous for its ancient woodlands and picturesque landscape that have inspired Romantic poets and artists including William Wordsworth and J.M.W. Turner – and form part of the border between England and Wales near Monmouth (Trefynwy). Further south, the Wye carves its way through a spectacular, deeply incised limestone gorge in a series of tight bends to reach Chepstow (Cas-gwent). To the east of the river, the Forest of Dean was once used as a royal hunting ground by Norman and Tudor kings. It is now the area's main mountain biking hub, with a huge network of bridleways, disused railway lines, forest tracks and the popular Forest of Dean Cycle Centre to explore.

ROUTE OVERVIEW
Ideal for a relaxed summer weekend, this leisurely route continually crosses back and forth over the border as it follows the River Wye north out of Chepstow, first on the newly opened Wye Valley Greenway and then on a mixture of forest tracks, bridleways and quiet lanes to Monmouth – all with minimal height gain. Highlights include an entertaining pedal through the kilometre-long Tidenham Tunnel, the option to explore the magnificent Gothic ruins of Tintern Abbey and the iconic view from the top of Symonds Yat Rock. From here, the route heads east into the Forest of Dean to sample some of its mellow family trails, flowy purpose-built singletrack and easy gravel tracks.

NAVIGATION
The route mainly sticks to waymarked trails including the Wye Valley Greenway, Sustrans routes 42 and 423 (Peregrine Path), and the mountain bike trails in the Forest of Dean. The trail leading to the Lower Redbrook to Wyesham disused railway line is easy to miss – look out for a small gap in the trees on the right, 100 metres after the Upper Redbrook turning. This is not officially a right of way, but the track is widely used by local cyclists to miss out the nearby A road and is part of plans for improving cycling infrastructure in the local area.

Wireworks Bridge, Tintern © RK.

GRADE ▲ **DISTANCE** 95.5km/59.3 miles **ASCENT** 1,220m/4,003ft **TERRAIN** 85% off-road, with a mix of flat forest tracks, bridleways, disused railways and quiet lanes, plus some flowy MTB trails **START/FINISH** Chepstow railway station **START/FINISH GRID REFERENCE** ST 536936 **BIKE-FRIENDLY PUBLIC TRANSPORT** At the start/finish **SATNAV** NP16 5PB **MAP** OS Explorer OL14, Wye Valley & Forest of Dean (1:25,000) **RECOMMENDED BIKE** Gravel bike

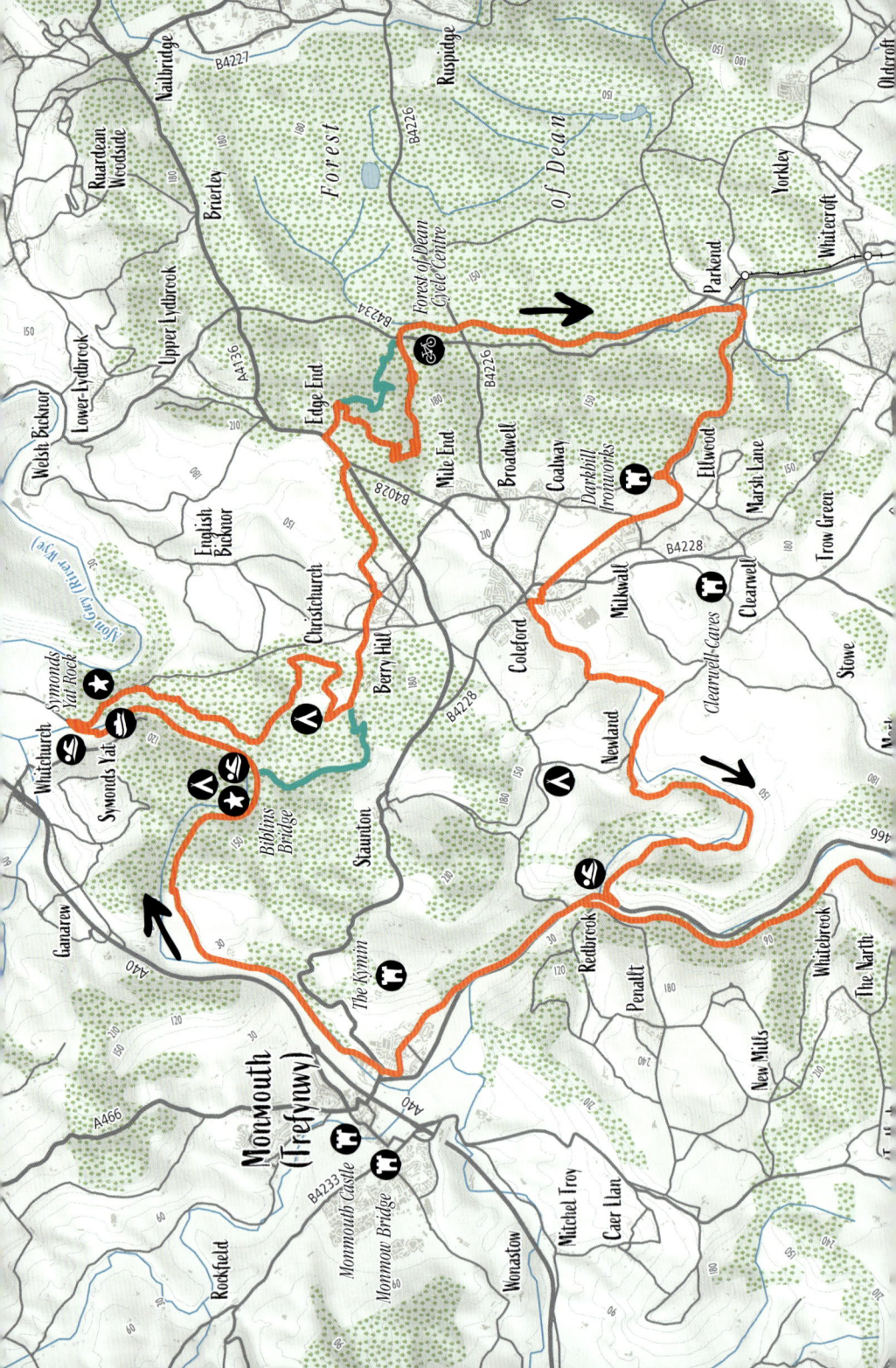

THE ROUTE

'If you have never navigated the Wye, you have seen nothing.'
William Gilpin, *Observations on the River Wye* (1782)

The River Wye is the longest river gorge in Wales, the fifth longest river in Britain and is designated as a Site of Special Scientific Interest (SSSI) along its entire length, one of only a few British rivers to receive this designation. One of the nation's favourite rivers, it is effectively one enormous, linear ecosystem – a long watery wildlife corridor through the Wye Valley AONB and an important breeding area for many different species. It is also one of the few rivers in England and Wales where an Act of Parliament has enshrined the right to navigate and swim in its lower reaches.

In many ways, a number of protections that the Wye now enjoys can be traced back to one man: the Reverend William Gilpin. In the summer of 1770, Gilpin embarked on the 'Picturesque Wye Tour' – a two-day excursion between Ross-on-Wye and Chepstow by boat – and he was so delighted by the scenery that he went on to write his *Observations on the River Wye* some years later.

Its publication was wildly successful: tourists came in their thousands to marvel at the picturesque landscape from the water, clamber up to specially created viewpoints to observe the river's 'mazy course', and explore the crumbling ruins along the riverbanks. Gilpin's writing fundamentally changed how people viewed the landscape, and arguably helped develop our ideas around the appreciation and conservation of natural places.

This bikepacking route takes you on a 'Picturesque Wye Tour' of your own, starting in Chepstow and working its way north towards Ross-on-Wye. As the route crosses the river for the first time over the Old Wye Bridge, there is a great view of Chepstow Castle perched right on the edge of the cliffs above the water, before the river disappears out of sight round a tight bend hemmed in by wooded banks and sheer limestone walls.

At Tutshill, the route joins the Wye Valley Greenway, a new traffic-free cycling route that uses the track bed of the old Wye Valley Railway. When it was opened in 1876, the railway helped renew interest in the Wye Tour almost a century after Gilpin first visited. The Tidenham Tunnel was reopened with the help

WHEN TO RIDE

The route primarily makes use of well-surfaced and smooth gravel paths, forest tracks and quiet lanes which can be ridden all year. The grassy bridleway between Brockweir and Bigsweir bridges is the only section which doesn't hold up as well in the winter months. There is an RSPB viewing point on Symonds Yat Rock where you can watch nesting peregrine falcons between April and August.

WARNINGS

The route follows the Wye Valley Greenway through the Tidenham Tunnel which is narrow and dimly lit – please keep to the left and turn off bike lights to avoid disturbing the bats. At the time of writing, the tunnel is open from 1 April to 30 September during the daytime – www.wyevalleygreenway.org; a diversion is shown on the map (with an accompanying GPX file) for when the tunnel is closed. The Wireworks Bridge was shut for repairs at the start of 2023 but is now open. Swimming in the Wye south of Bigsweir Bridge is dangerous due to the tidal waters.

L–R: *View from Symonds Yat Rock* © RK; *mural on the Globe Inn, Coleford; Penallt Viaduct (Redbrook Railway Bridge)* © RK; *Offa's Dyke Path between Brockweir and Bigsweir* © Will Kingston-Budge.

WATER
Despite the route closely following the River Wye, there are few places to fill up. It's best to use the many cafes and pubs along the way.

FOOD AND DRINK
- The Filling Station Cafe, Tintern (tools, bike pump and spares also available). T: 07770 544 592
- The Anchor Inn, Tintern. T: 01291 689 582
- The Old Station Tintern, Tintern Heights (seasonal). T: 01291 689 566
- The Boat Inn, Penallt. T: 01600 712 615
- Redbrook Village Stores, Redbrook. T: 01600 772 488
- Pedalabikeaway Cafe, Forest of Dean Cycle Centre. T: 01594 729 000
- The Ostrich Inn, Newland. T: 01594 833 260

The town of Monmouth is just off-route with plenty of larger shops to choose from.

ACCOMMODATION
- Camping at The Old Station Tintern, Tintern Heights (seasonal). T: 01291 689 566
- Beeches Farm Campsite, Tidenham Chase. T: 07791 540 016
- Ferry Farm Camping, Tintern. T: 07984 008 372
- YHA St Briavels Castle, St Briavels. T: 0345 371 9042
- Cherry Orchard Campsite, Newland. T: 01594 810 413

of an army of volunteers, and it burrows through the hard limestone rock for over a kilometre.

After the tunnel, the route continues on slightly rougher forestry tracks north to Tintern Abbey (£), one of the main features of the Wye Tour. Even after falling victim to the Dissolution of the Monasteries in 1536, much of the abbey's tracery and intricate stonework remain remarkably intact, including its huge west front and window. First founded in 1131, the Cistercian monks chose to build Tintern Abbey here both for the tranquillity of the valley and the proximity of the Wye. By the time the first tourists floated past on the Wye Tour, the area would have looked very different. It is hard to imagine that by 1600 Tintern was home to the largest industrial enterprise in Wales. The riverbanks would have been lined with iron, copper and tin works belching smoke into the valley, and much of the surrounding woodland would have been cut down to feed the area's lime kilns and furnaces.

Further up the Wye, the route shifts back and forth between England and Wales as it crosses Brockweir Bridge, Bigsweir Bridge and then Redbrook Bridge. The off-road section between the first two bridges follows a scenic bridleway right along the banks of the river, alternating between open, grassy singletrack and dappled trails. The Wye has long enjoyed a reputation for being one of the least polluted rivers in England and Wales despite its industrial past, and the water looks clean enough from here. However, water samples and giant algae blooms in recent years tell a very different story. The river is a Special Area of Conservation (SAC), yet high levels of damaging phosphates have been found in the river and are thought to be caused by a combination of raw sewage and manure from intensive poultry farming. Many people still enjoy canoeing and swimming in the Wye though; use common sense and have a

look at The Rivers Trust online sewage map before taking a dip: *www.theriverstrust.org/sewage-map*

Near Monmouth – birthplace of Henry V – the route joins the excellent Peregrine Path (Sustrans Route 423) on compacted gravel to reach Symonds Yat. There are a number of historic riverside pubs to enjoy, including the Saracens Head and the Ye Old Ferrie Inn; both pubs have their own hand-pulled ferries that operate across the river for a small fee. They even take bikes. From here, there is a steep road climb up from the river to reach the famous viewpoint at Symonds Yat Rock, where the Wye forms an almost complete loop below.

The route then heads east to the Forest of Dean Cycle Centre (formerly the Cannop Cycle Centre). From the Norman Conquest in 1066 until 1971, this land was a Royal Forest – it was used by Norman kings as their personal hunting ground. Verderers were appointed to act for the king and protect his rights, while in the 14th century Edward I established the rights of Freeminers – an ancient title given to coal or iron miners in the Forest of Dean. There are a number of options here depending on what you feel like riding, including two purpose-built mountain biking trails – the Freeminers Trail (red) and the Verderers Trail (blue) – as well as a huge network of well-surfaced forest tracks and disused railway lines that work their way around a labyrinth of rifts, hollows and deep pits known locally as *scowles*.

The return leg of the route rejoins the river at Lower Redbrook to retrace the Wye Tour back to Chepstow. Travellers in search of the Picturesque always had some essential items in their luggage to view and record the landscapes they encountered, but consider swapping out your curved Claude glass, tinted plates, barometer and telescope for a bivvy bag, swimming kit and snacks, to ensure the best bikepacking experience along the Wye.

- Bracelands Campsite, Coleford.
  T: 01594 837 258
- Biblins Youth Campsite, Biblins Bridge (available during school holidays only).
  T: 01600 890 850

OTHER ROUTES NEARBY

Consider starting from Bristol for a longer trip – follow Sustrans Route 4 over the 1.6-kilometre Severn Bridge and into Chepstow. A planning application has been submitted for the Dean Forest Greenway, a traffic-free route between Parkend and Lydney. More information can be found at *www.greenwaysandcycleroutes.org*

BIKE SHOPS AND HIRE

- Pedalabikeaway Cycle Centre, Cannop Valley. T: 01594 729 000
- Dean Forest Cycles, Parkend.
  T: 01594 368 009
- Ace Bicycles, Monmouth.
  T: 01600 715 071
- Launch Bikes, Monmouth.
  T: 01600 772 775
- Wye-Bikes, Coleford. T: 07856 597 044

SUPPORT

The Dean Trail Volunteers help develop and maintain the official mountain bike trails in the Forest of Dean:
www.deantrailvolunteers.org.uk

Consider volunteering/donating to help maintain the Wye Valley Greenway and keep the Tidenham Tunnel open:
www.wyevalleygreenway.org

L-R: *Biblins Bridge © RK; Tintern Abbey © RK.*

08 THE TRANS CAMBRIAN WAY

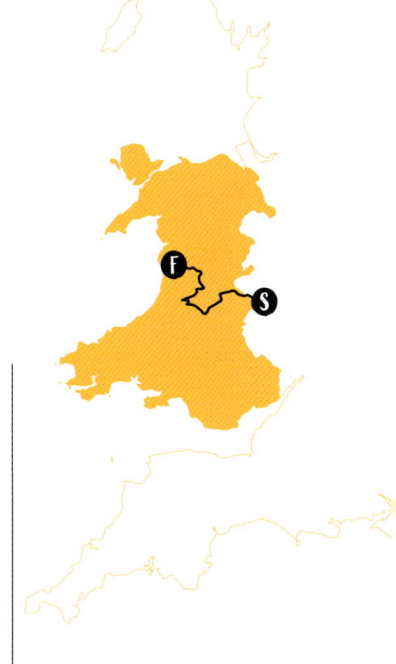

INTRODUCTION

Originally applied in a general sense to most of upland Wales, the Cambrian Mountains has come to describe the wild and remote landscape found between Eryri (Snowdonia) and Bannau Brycheiniog (Brecon Beacons) – a great watershed right in the heart of Wales. These mountains are some of the oldest in the world and form the backbone of the country. The area is effectively one enormous upland plateau – smooth and undulating rather than jagged and steep-sided for the most part – and is made up of three distinct areas: the Pumlumon massif to the north near Machynlleth, the central range known as Elenydd, and Mynydd Mallaen to the south. Sparsely populated, crossed by only a handful of lonely roads and passed over by the tourist hordes in favour of Wales's national parks, the Cambrian Mountains offer bikepackers a sense of true remoteness, emptiness and tranquillity that is rare to find this far south in Britain.

ROUTE OVERVIEW

The Trans Cambrian Way is one of Wales's most well-known and popular multi-day off-road routes, and deservedly so. Developed by Jeremy Atkinson and UK members of the International Mountain Bike Association, this linear route takes riders on a challenging but unforgettable adventure across the country. The route snakes its way around the Cambrian Mountains, starting from Knighton (Tref-y-Clawdd) on the border between England and Wales and finishing on the coast at the Dyfi Estuary. It dips into remote valleys and doubles back on itself in order to squeeze in as many quality trails as it can,

Previous page: Descending from the Pumlumon escarpment © RK. (route 08).
Skirting under Foel Fadian © RK.

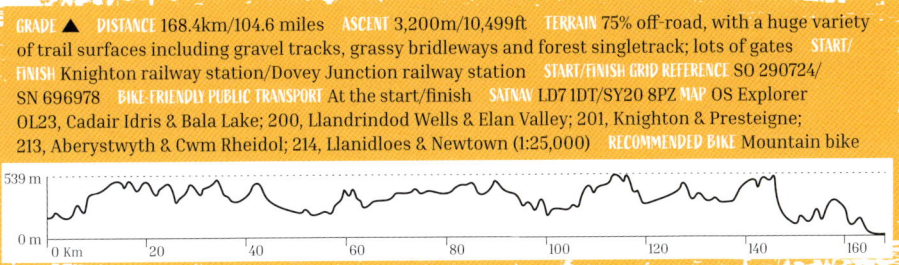

GRADE ▲ **DISTANCE** 168.4km/104.6 miles **ASCENT** 3,200m/10,499ft **TERRAIN** 75% off-road, with a huge variety of trail surfaces including gravel tracks, grassy bridleways and forest singletrack; lots of gates **START/FINISH** Knighton railway station/Dovey Junction railway station **START/FINISH GRID REFERENCE** SO 290724/SN 696578 **BIKE-FRIENDLY PUBLIC TRANSPORT** At the start/finish **SATNAV** LD7 1DT/SY20 8PZ **MAP** OS Explorer OL23, Cadair Idris & Bala Lake; 200, Llandrindod Wells & Elan Valley; 201, Knighton & Presteigne; 213, Aberystwyth & Cwm Rheidol; 214, Llanidloes & Newtown (1:25,000) **RECOMMENDED BIKE** Mountain bike

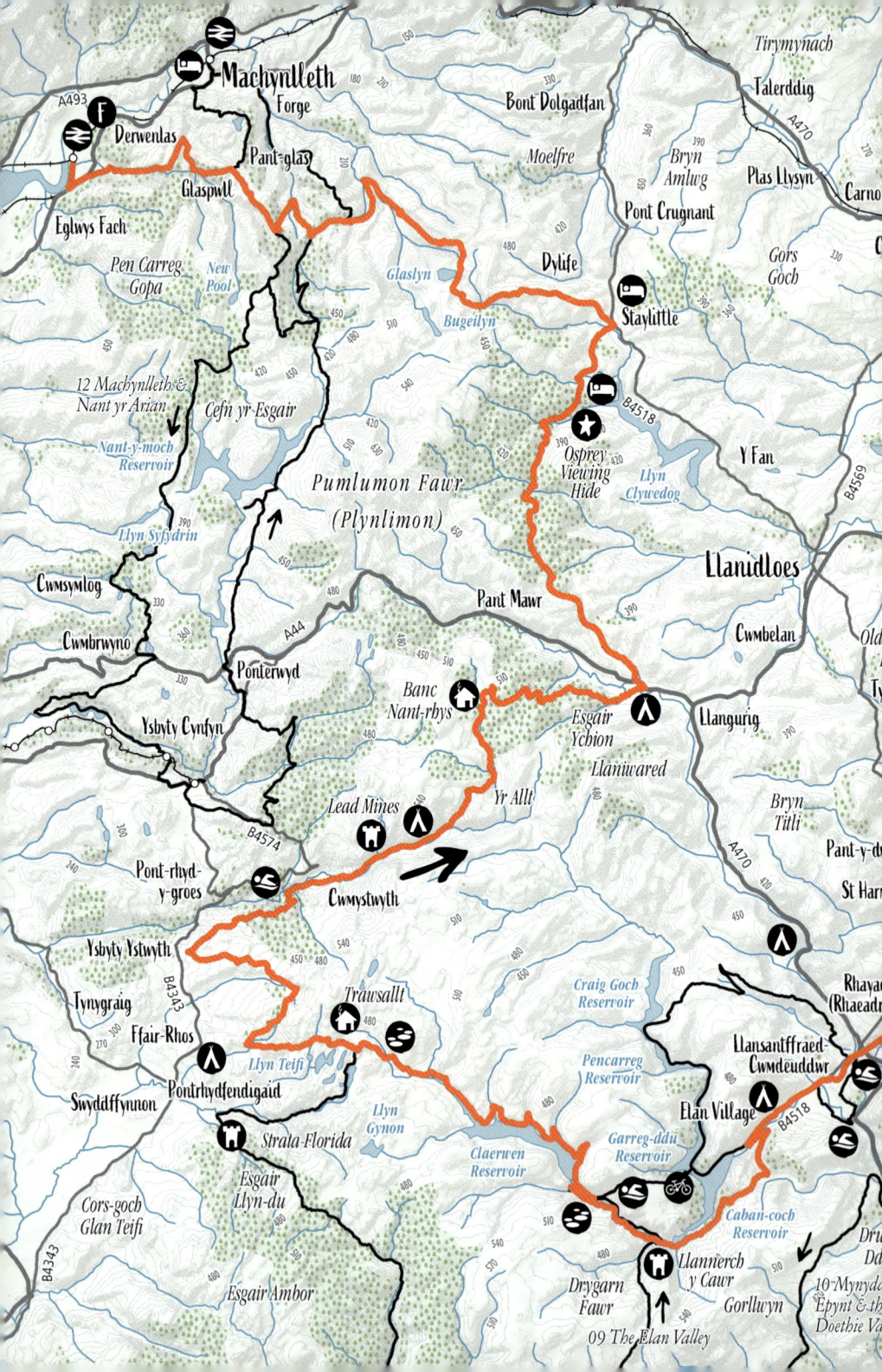

and in the process the route racks up some serious elevation. It also passes through many of the most scenic landscapes in Mid Wales including the Elan Valley, Teifi Pools and the Hafod Estate, and goes past several excellent bothies. Most riders complete the route in three days with overnight stops near Rhayader (Rhaeadr Gwy) and Llangurig, but four days are recommended for a more relaxed ride.

THE ROUTE

'Cut by deep wooded valleys and gorges, their rolling moor lands are colourful at all seasons and are one of Britain's loveliest ... countrysides [sic] .... attracting discerning visitors in increasing numbers who appreciate that this 'spirit of Wales' is the equal in beauty of many existing national parks.'
Countryside Commission (1972)

Bikepackers are some of the Cambrian Mountains' newest 'discerning visitors'. This remote and sparsely populated region is sometimes called the Green Desert of Wales – a homogenous, uninterrupted expanse of rolling moorland – but the Trans Cambrian Way reveals a much more varied and nuanced landscape, and each section of the route has a very distinctive feel. Riding here, it is hard to believe that this region of Wales is not better recognised or protected. It came very close, first in 1965 when the National Parks Commission decided that the Cambrian Mountains should become Britain's next national park, and then again in 1972 when the Countryside Commission made a national park designation order that was rejected by the Secretary of State for Wales the following year. Over 50 years later, the Cambrian Mountains is still one of Wales's most special places – a peaceful, largely unspoiled landscape with a rich cultural history and astounding natural beauty.

Starting in Knighton, the Trans Cambrian Way follows the River Teme on quiet country lanes before the route's first big ascent out of Knucklas (Cnwclas). It climbs above an impressive viaduct around Castle Hill and then immediately loses all its hard-won height, dropping down to Lloyney for an even steeper climb on to Pool Hill. A sunken holloway leads up through the woods and then it's a prolonged, steep push up a grassy

NAVIGATION

This route is not officially waymarked. However, look out for small yellow arrows painted on gates and signposts – infrequent but reassuring. There is one official wooden signpost just before Storehouse (SN 752722) at the start of the restricted byway down to Dologau. The end of the Trans Cambrian Way joins part of the 'Mach' MTB routes which have been newly waymarked.

WHEN TO RIDE

Most of the trails hold up well all year round, although the first section between Knighton and Rhayader is predominantly grass based. Transport logistics, rather than the weather, may well dictate when you ride this linear route – it finishes at Dovey Junction railway station but there is no direct train back to Knighton. Either take the train via Shrewsbury or arrange for a company to shuttle you back to the start. Mountain Bike Wales specialises in guiding riders along the Trans Cambrian Way – www.mtb.wales

L–R: *Claerwen Dam © RK; scenic gravel around Claerwen Reservoir © RK; on the 'Mohawk Road' out of Cwm Ystwyth; wind turbines near Warren Hill © RK; brew at Claerddu bothy © RK.*

WARNINGS

There are many river crossings on the route, although most have footbridges nearby. The ford at Llanbadarn Fynydd is easily avoided by a short detour to the nearby road bridge. The Sunken Road between Caban-coch and Claerwen reservoirs is aptly named as it becomes literally submerged after heavy rain – take the road on the opposite side of the valley to avoid it if needed. There is a locked gate at Brondre Fawr farm at the edge of the plantation (just north of Bwlch-y-sarnau) which bikes will need to be lifted over (grid reference: SO 035770).

WATER

There are numerous rivers to fill up from en route.

L–R: Caban-coch Reservoir © RK; Claerddu bothy © RK; MBA signage; springtime at Nant Rhys bothy.

bridleway to join Glyndŵr's Way National Trail. The views along the top are vast and empty as the route follows the fence line on close-cropped grass, with just the odd lone hawthorn tree and sheep for company.

Further west, there are sections of unexpected singletrack around Warren Hill – the riding is fast, grassy and little more than the width of a tyre in places – and there is an excellent descent down to Lower Green Farm. In spring, the farmhouse is surrounded by yellow daffodils and the fields are full of tiny newborn lambs. The tracks here are also bordered by some impressive examples of traditional Welsh 'living' fences. Look closely and you can see how these hedges have been skilfully laid: the tree branches (pleaches) have been partially cut at their base, enough to lay them at an angle but not too much so they can continue to grow, and then woven between vertical stakes. These hedges have spent years curving and twisting along the field boundaries and now they look as if they are flowing up the hillside.

The Trans Cambrian Way isn't known for picking the most direct route – that is half its charm – but west of Llanbadarn Fynydd it takes a very indirect wiggle through Brondre-fawr Hill plantation. There is some excellent singletrack in the trees, but this loop may feel too contrived for tired legs. Stay on the road if needed for a couple of kilometres to reach Bwlch-y-

sarnau and the wonderful Glyndŵr's Way Community Centre. There is drinking water available 24/7 in the porch area, along with a kettle, bike pump, bike tools and USB charging ports next to a donation box. Likewise, the market town of Rhayader is well worth exploring – pause here to stock up on supplies, play around on the pump track and swim in the river.

Just west of Rhayader, the route heads into Elenydd and the stunning flooded landscape of the Elan Valley. It is one of the highlights of the trip with five huge reservoirs, six ornate dams and dramatic, steep-sided valleys. The traffic-free Elan Valley Trail runs downhill all the way to the visitor centre and its new bike hub, before the route climbs sharply above the immense Caban-coch Reservoir. From up here, the reservoir seems to completely fill the valley floor, curving out of sight around corners, behind wooded hills and disappearing off into the distance to merge with Garreg-ddu Reservoir. The descent is a wonderfully long and drawn-out affair: it launches itself off the top on an open grassy bridleway past the old ruins of Ty'n-y-pant house, climbing a little up by a forestry plantation, before barrelling across the hillside under Gro Hill and finishing right by the water's edge. To reach Claerwen Dam, either tackle the infamous Sunken Road with its fun, testing rocky sections and deep puddles, or cross the bridge to take the optional route up the road on the opposite side of the river.

FOOD AND DRINK

- Castle Inn, Knucklas. T: 01547 528 150
- Llanbadarnfynydd Community Shop, Llanbadarn Fynydd (reduced opening hours at the weekend). T: 01597 840 448
- Glyndŵr's Way Porch Cafe, Bwlch-y-sarnau (seasonal; tea and coffee only).
- Elan Valley Visitor Centre Cafe. T: 01597 810 449
- Penbont House Tea Rooms, Elan Valley. T: 01597 811 515
- Strata Florida Abbey Visitor Centre, Ystrad Fflur (light refreshments only). T: 03000 252 239
- The Miners Arms, Pont-rhyd-y-groes. T: 01974 282 238
- The Village Tearoom, Llangurig. T: 07748 343 252
- Staylittle Post Office & Stores, Staylittle. T: 0345 722 3344

Rhayader has many options to stock up on supplies.

ACCOMMODATION

- Mid Wales Bunkhouse – Tipi and Camping, St Harmon. T: 07926 781 394
- Nannerth Country Holidays Wildcamp and Camping, Rhayader.
  T: 01597 811 121
- Elan Oaks Camping and Caravan Site, Elan Valley. T: 01597 810 326
- Claerddu Bothy (Elan Valley Trust)
  – www.elanvalley.org.uk
- Penrhiw Campsite, Ffair Rhos.
  T: 01974 831 408
- Tyllwyd Campsite, Pontarfynach.
  T: 01974 282 216
- Nant Rhys Bothy (Mountain Bothies Association) –
  www.mountainbothies.org.uk
- Glangwy Farm Campsite, Llanidloes.
  T: 07890 083 630
- Hafren Forest Hideaway, Staylittle.
  T: 07871 740 514
- The Lodge, Staylittle. T: 07790 761 859
- Toad Hall, Machynlleth.
  T: 01654 700 597

Claerwen Dam marks the start of one of Wales's finest gravel roads. It follows the northern edge of the reservoir on pale, potholed gravel for almost 10 deserted kilometres before turning into a lonely singletrack road. This area feels more isolated and remote than the first half of the route as it works its way north past the Teifi Pools. The delightful Claerddu bothy, managed by the Elan Valley Trust, is tucked away at the end of a faint track on the right.

After a fabulous singletrack descent through Coed Bwlch-gwallter, the route briefly dips into the Hafod Estate before climbing up through Cwm Ystwyth. People have long been drawn to the area because of its mineral wealth – silver, lead, zinc and copper have all been mined here since Roman times – and there is evidence of mining activity as far back as the Bronze Age. Archaeologists even discovered the rare gold Banc Ty'nddôl sun-disc in a grave near Copa Hill, high up on the valley's northern slope. Cwm Ystwyth is windswept and quiet now, but it would have been a flurry of human activity in the late 1800s. Look out for the ruined stone buildings either side of the road which were built to process the ore mined from the hillside and to provide houses for the workers.

North of Nant Rhys bothy and Llangurig, the route begins its final stage across the Pumlumon massif. There's more superb, narrow singletrack along the banks of Afon Bidno,

a chance to see ospreys (and ride some off-piste singletrack) in Hafren Forest and one last opportunity to stock up on supplies in Staylittle (Penffordd-Lâs) before the route heads back up into the mountains. The route follows Glyndŵr's Way on a fantastic, exposed bridleway above the Clywedog gorge to reach Glaslyn lake and the biggest descent of the Trans Cambrian Way. Dropping off the massif's dramatic northern escarpment, it follows the fence line above a ravine before tackling a steep series of sketchy zigzags covered in loose rock below Foel Fadian. At the gate, the trail mellows out and finishes on a long grassy run-out to the road.

The last section of any long-distance route is tough, but the Trans Cambrian Way has an added sting in its tail. It feels like it should be all downhill to the coast, but there are plenty of punchy climbs left before you reach the Dyfi Estuary. Some riders understandably opt to finish in Machynlleth instead, however there are some real gems that make the last hills worth it if you have any energy left. The singletrack above the Afon Hengwm gorge is a real highlight, as is the descent off Bwlch y Groesen with views across to the enormous waterfall of Pistyll y Llyn. A final relaxed spin down the scenic Llyfnant Valley delivers riders to the edge of the Dyfi Estuary, a handful of houses and a train station in the middle of nowhere. It is an oddly fitting end to such a memorable, remote ride.

OTHER ROUTES NEARBY

The Ystwyth Trail is a 34-kilometre route between Aberystwyth and Tregaron and offers a good bail-out option if needed – after Claerwen Reservoir, continue west to join the trail at Ystradmeurig. Follow signs for Sustrans Route 82 and then route 81 to reach the coast.

BIKE SHOPS AND HIRE

- Clive Powell Bikes, Rhayader.
  T: 01597 811 343
- Neil's Wheels, Rhayader.
  T: 07495 919 508
- Elan Valley Visitor Centre & Bike Hub, Elan Village. T: 01597 810 880. Located at the Elan Valley visitor centre, there are bike washing facilities, a bike workshop, changing cubicles, toilets and a cafe on site.

L–R: Singletrack below Gro Hill © RK; the end of the Trans Cambrian Way.

09 THE ELAN VALLEY

INTRODUCTION

The Elan Valley – often dubbed the 'Lake District of Wales' – sits right at the heart of Elenydd in the middle of the Cambrian Mountains. It is a beautiful landscape of remote hills, isolated farms and steep-sided valleys, but for many visitors the area's biggest draw is its five immense reservoirs that were built to supply clean water to Birmingham. The Elan Valley is also one of the heartlands of Welsh language and culture. On its western edge, the ruined abbey at Strata Florida (Ystrad Fflur) is an internationally significant site that was once an important centre of culture, religion and trade with connections spreading far across the Welsh landscape. The market town of Rhayader (Rhaeadr Gwy) to the east, meanwhile, is home to a pump track, some great swimming spots and the famous Red Kite Feeding Centre at Gigrin Farm. With its International Dark Sky Park status, numerous bothies and old droving roads, the Elan Valley is the perfect place to disappear on a weekend adventure.

ROUTE OVERVIEW

Starting in Rhayader, this route focuses on the world-class network of trails surrounding the Elan Valley and its reservoirs. Working its way west, it joins the scenic Elan Valley Trail before skirting around Claerwen Reservoir to reach the Teifi Pools and the brilliant Cwm Egnant descent down to Strata Florida and the ruins of its abbey. A tough road climb over the Devil's Staircase, a cruise down the stunning Irfon Valley and a wild, isolated crossing over Abergwesyn Common lead back east to rejoin the flooded valleys and the new flow trails at Nantgwyllt.

Sunset over Craig Goch Reservoir © RK.

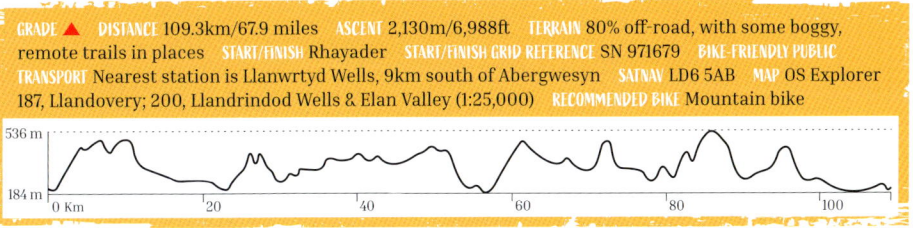

GRADE ▲ **DISTANCE** 109.3km/67.9 miles **ASCENT** 2,130m/6,988ft **TERRAIN** 80% off-road, with some boggy, remote trails in places **START/FINISH** Rhayader **START/FINISH GRID REFERENCE** SN 971679 **BIKE-FRIENDLY PUBLIC TRANSPORT** Nearest station is Llanwrtyd Wells, 9km south of Abergwesyn **SATNAV** LD6 5AB **MAP** OS Explorer 187, Llandovery; 200, Llandrindod Wells & Elan Valley (1:25,000) **RECOMMENDED BIKE** Mountain bike

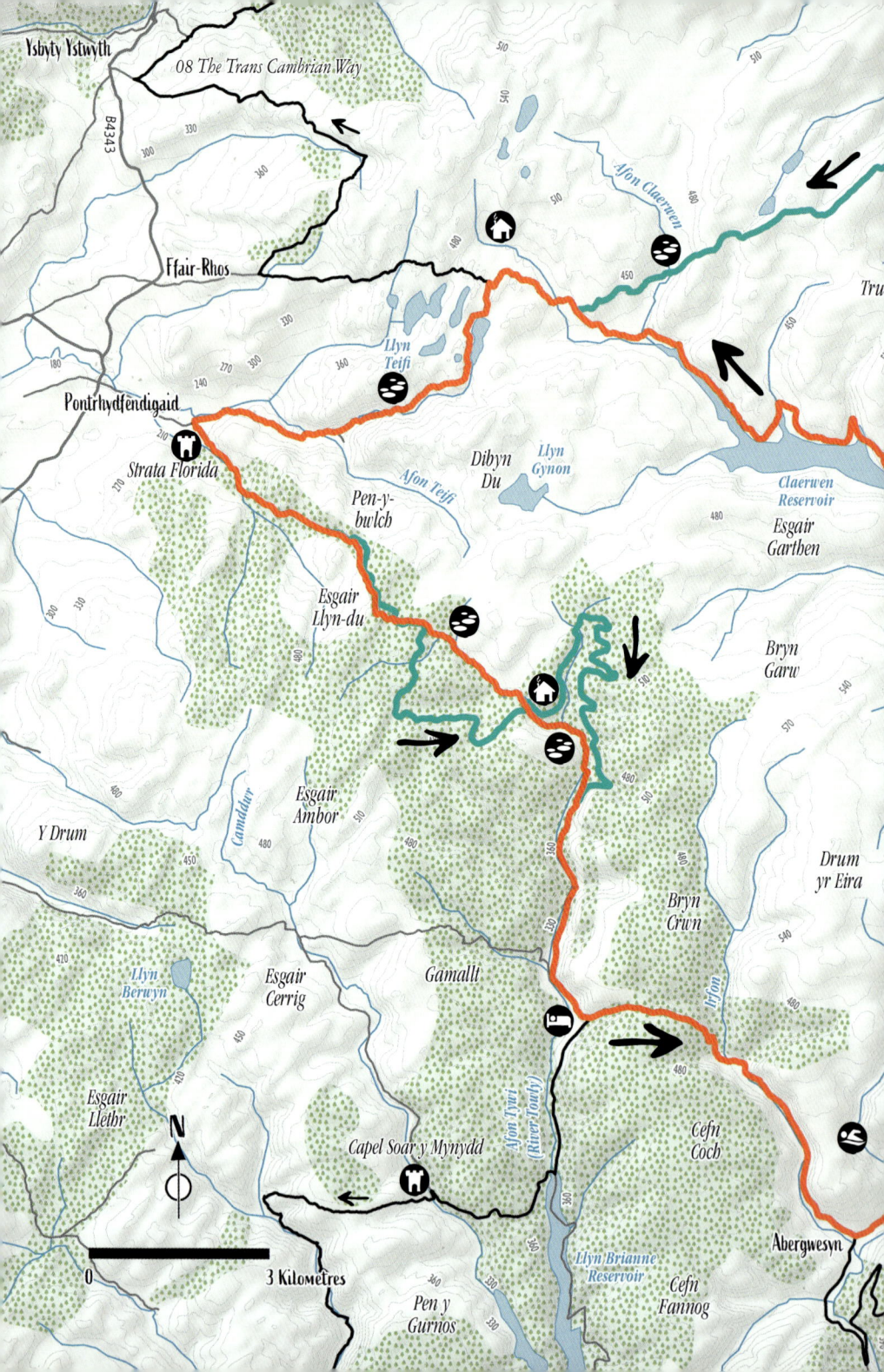

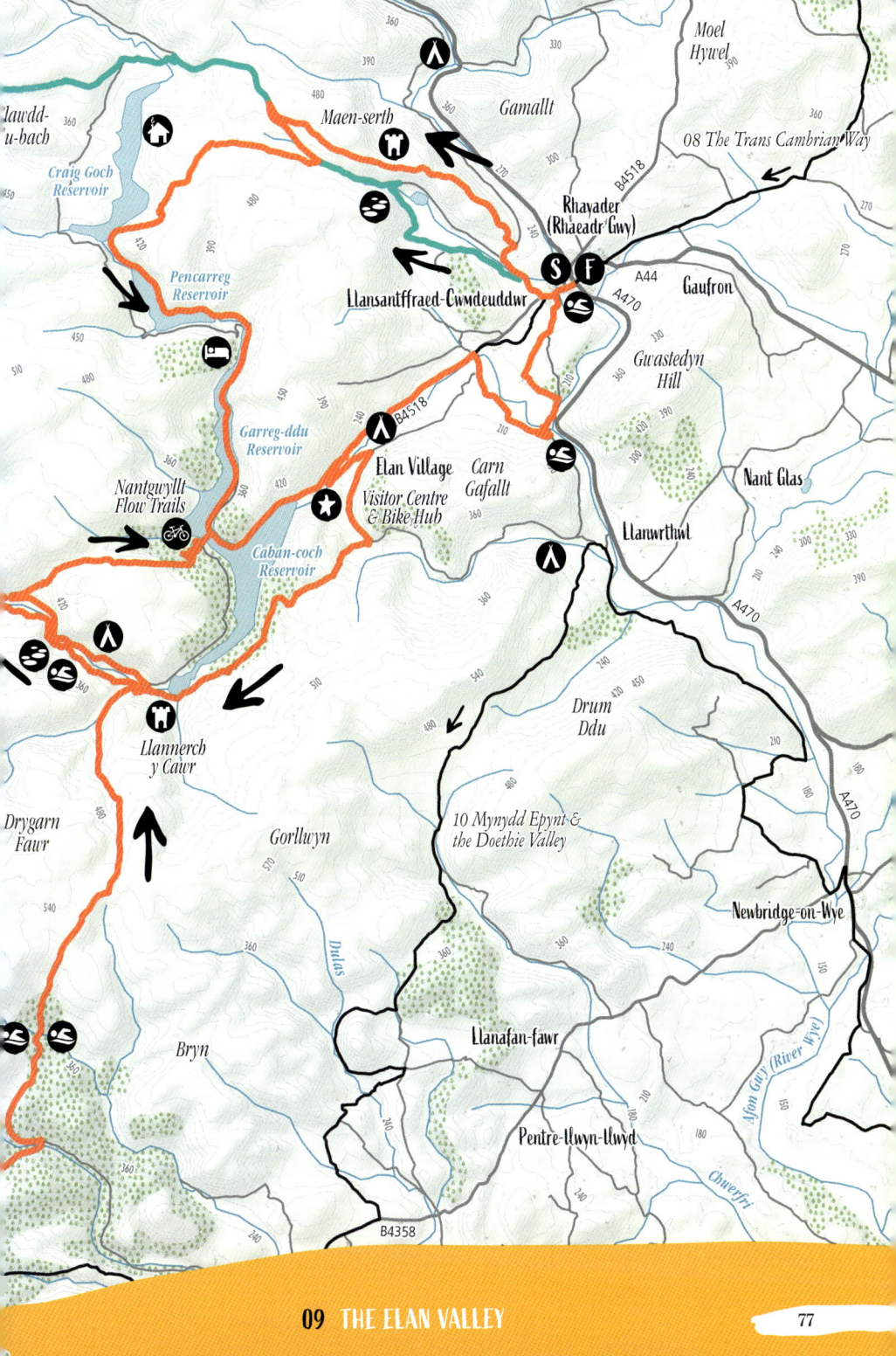

There is also an optional challenging crossing on the historic medieval road known as the Monks' Trod (Llwybr y Mynaich), which passes over a wonderful stretch of very remote and little-visited moorland between Nannerth and Strata Florida. The boggy byway won't be most riders' cup of tea, but it offers a unique experience for bikepackers wanting to better understand the area's history and find some real solitude.

THE ROUTE

It is April and patches of snow still linger on the higher trails across Elenydd despite the day's warmth. The old shepherd's cottage at Lluest Cwmbach is a welcome sight, its chimney spotted first from the faint sheep track above Craig Goch Reservoir before the rest of the bothy comes into view. Inside, a black and white framed photo of Mick Jagger sits propped up on a window ledge opposite a well-used dartboard. Outside, a bench runs along the back wall of the cottage and looks out across the still, glassy expanse of water – perfect for soaking up the last of the sun with an early dinner.

The high, exposed moorland of Elenydd has long been used for upland farming, and the remains of farm cottages, huts and sheepfolds dot the area. Traditionally, farmers would have followed the seasonal 'Hafod a Hendre' system with the sheep staying low down in the sheltered pastures during the winter months and then being taken to graze on the higher mountains in the summer. Riding across Elenydd, it quickly becomes apparent how the rural communities and their livelihoods are still closely tied to the land; farming here must be a hard existence, but a rewarding one. The same could be said for bikepacking here.

The route starts in the pretty market town of Rhayader – the first town on the River Wye and the oldest in Mid Wales – right in the middle of an important crossroads. In the 18th and 19th centuries, drovers would have passed by the town with their animals on their way to the English markets in the east, and the town also became a key staging post on the coach road from Aberystwyth to London (now the busy A44). Its historic pubs and inns are a clear legacy; look out for the Old Swan,

NAVIGATION

The main route uses bridleways and byways which are very remote but fairly obvious on the ground. The exposed moorland crossing over Abergwesyn Common is the exception – the trail is faint and boggy in places as it climbs up to a prominent cairn at the top of Nant Paradwys. The final section of the Cwm Egnant bridleway has been diverted over a footbridge to avoid Tyncwm farm near Strata Florida.

WHEN TO RIDE

The Elan Valley area is one of the wettest parts of the British Isles. The Sunken Road byway between Caban-coch and Claerwen reservoirs is aptly named as it can become completely submerged after heavy rain, but it can be easily avoided by taking the road instead. The track between Strata Florida and the Devil's Staircase through Tywi Forest has many fords and deep puddles to cross as well – these can be avoided using the forestry roads either side of the track.

L–R: *Rhayader; sunrise over Craig Goch Reservoir © RK; Garreg Ddu dam © RK; bridleway above Craig Goch Reservoir.*

WARNINGS

The Elan Valley Trail between Craig Goch Dam and Penygarreg Dam is now open, having been closed for a number of years due to a large rockfall in Devil's Gulch. Lluest Cwmbach bothy can be tricky to reach in late summer due to the high bracken. The optional Monks' Trod is as wild, remote and committing as it gets in Wales; it starts off promisingly, climbing on a good track above Pont ar Elan before following a line of wooden stakes across boggy moorland for over five kilometres. There is some solid doubletrack near Llyn Cerrigllwydion before an even wetter final section between Rhyd Hengae ford and Teifi Pools.

L–R: *Golf Links byway, upper Elan Valley; climbing up to Bwlch y Ddau Faen; snowy singletrack above Nant Paradwys; bothy fire preparations; Moel Prysgau bothy; Nantgwyllt flow trails.*

the Cwmdauddwr Arms, the Lion Royal Hotel and the charming 16th-century Triangle Inn by the river.

Leaving Rhayader, the route climbs steeply out of the upper Elan Valley and over towards Craig Goch Reservoir. There are two options here: either stay on a scenic bridleway up through the valley before crossing Nant Gwynllyn at a small waterfall (this is shown on the map as an optional route) or follow the old drove road on the opposite side of the valley past Maen-serth standing stone. Reaching over two metres high, the stone may well have been used as a marker by drovers travelling across Elenydd from Cwmystwyth to Rhayader.

Rhayader is often called the gateway to the Elan Valley, yet it is still remarkable how quickly the agricultural landscape around the town morphs into a secret world of flooded valleys, ornate dams and ancient woodland. After climbing up through the middle of a Roman marching camp, the route descends on a fast, grassy bridleway towards Lluest Cwmbach bothy and Craig Goch Reservoir. This was one of five reservoirs built by the Birmingham Corporation to provide the rapidly expanding city with clean drinking water under the Water Act of 1892. While the compulsory purchase of the Elan and Claerwen valleys created this spectacular new landscape, like many water schemes in Wales it was highly controversial. Tenant farmers were evicted without any financial compensation and their

homes and livelihoods were lost under the water along with two manor houses, the village school and a church.

At Craig Goch Reservoir, the route joins the scenic Elan Valley Trail on a disused railway line that once transported dam workers and building materials around the site. The trail winds its way gradually down through the reservoir system and passes one impressive feat of Victorian engineering after another, each one a lesson in Victorian fantasy Baroque architecture. Craig Goch Dam is the area's most-photographed dam with its series of arches, elegantly curved retaining wall, and copper-roofed valve tower, while Caban-coch Dam looks very plain in comparison. When the reservoir is full, though, the water pours over the huge concrete dam and transforms it into a wall of white water.

Past the visitor centre and its new bike hub, the route joins the Trans Cambrian Way (page 65) to climb up high above Caban-coch Reservoir for a fabulous descent off Gro Hill. Further north, the infamous Sunken Road follows the Afon Claerwen up to the final reservoir and introduces a number of technical sections for riders to tackle, including some short climbs over stepped bedrock and plenty of puddles that practically guarantee wet feet all year round.

Above Claerwen Dam, the route follows the northern edge of the reservoir on deserted gravel for almost 10 kilometres.

WATER

There are numerous places to fill up from en route if needed. All three bothies on the route are next to accessible streams or rivers.

FOOD AND DRINK

- Triangle Inn, Rhayader.
  T: 01597 810 537
- The Old Swan Tea Rooms, Rhayader.
  T: 01597 811 060
- Penbont House Tea Rooms, Elan Valley.
  T: 01597 811 515
- Elan Valley Visitor Centre Cafe.
  T: 01597 810 449
- Strata Florida Abbey Visitor Centre, Ystrad Fflur (light refreshments only).
  T: 03000 252 239
- Red Lion Hotel, Pontrhydfendigaid.
  T: 01974 831 547

At the far end of the water, it leaves the Trans Cambrian Way just before the track to Claerddu bothy and follows a remote access road along the edge of the Teifi Pools. One of the larger pools – Llyn Egnant – marks the start of one of the most memorable descents of the route: an open, grassy bridleway leisurely descends to reach the head of Cwm Egnant, before narrowing to become a thin strip of gravel singletrack racing through the bracken as the sides of the valley start to close in. The grass is soon replaced by bedrock as the route picks its way down the steepening hillside, splashing through small streams with only the occasional gate to break up the flow, before reaching a footbridge and the road.

Heading north, the route passes Strata Florida and the ruins of its 12th-century Cistercian abbey (£). Known as the 'Westminster of Wales', the abbey was once one of the most celebrated religious buildings in Wales, a place of pilgrimage and a cornerstone of Welsh culture. A yew tree in the churchyard is believed to mark the grave of the medieval Welsh poet, Dafydd ap Gwilym. The Cistercian monks chose this beautiful and remote valley for quiet contemplation and prayer – Strata Florida is a Latinisation of the Welsh Ystrad Fflur ('Valley of Flowers') – but they also saw the land's potential to generate a lot of wealth. The Teifi Pools were used to farm eels and brown trout, wool was traded at Ffair Rhos, and the nearby village of Pontrhydfendigaid ('Bridge at the Holy Ford') was built to house the abbey's mineworkers.

Considering the abbey's location, the monks were surprisingly well connected. Strata Florida was linked with neighbouring

Cwmhir Abbey via the medieval road known as the Monks' Trod (Llwybr y Mynaich), and much of the road's original construction has survived because of its remote setting. Nowadays, riders can traverse the Monks' Trod (shown on the map as an alternative route and available as a GPX file) to get a sense of what it was like to cross the wild Elenydd many centuries ago, but be prepared for some serious type-2 fun.

The final section of the route gradually works its way back over to the Elan Valley, first tackling the steep road climb known as the Devil's Staircase before an outrageously scenic cruise down the Irfon Valley. Past Abergwesyn Village Hall, the route begins the climb over Abergwesyn Common on a wild and committing bridleway up Esgair yr Ŵyn ('Ridge of the Lambs'). It is boggy and pretty faint in places, but there are wonderful views out to Drygarn Fawr and its two large beehive-shaped cairns. The singletrack descent down Nant Paradwys is more than adequate consolation too. The route finishes with a play on the new flow trails above Nantgwyllt Church before returning to Rhayader.

ACCOMMODATION
- Nannerth Country Holidays Wildcamp and Camping, Rhayader. T: 01597 811 121
- Penbont House B&B, Elan Valley. T: 01597 811 515
- Elan Oaks Camping and Caravan Site, Elan Valley. T: 01597 810 326
- Cwm Clyd Bunkhouse, Claerwen Valley. T: 01597 810 449
- Claerddu Bothy (Elan Valley Trust) – www.elanvalley.org.uk
- Moel Prysgau Bothy (Mountain Bothies Association) – www.mountainbothies.org.uk
- Lluest Cwmbach Bothy (Mountain Bothies Association) – www.mountainbothies.org.uk
- Dolgoch Hostel, Tregaron. T: 01440 730 226
- Doliago Farm Campsite, Llanwrthwl. T: 07870 537 179

OTHER ROUTES NEARBY
The Ystwyth Trail is a 34-kilometre, largely off-road route between Aberystwyth and Tregaron which passes near Strata Florida. The Coed Trallwm mountain bike trails are now closed to the public and are only available for guests staying in the on-site holiday cottages.

BIKE SHOPS AND HIRE
- Clive Powell Bikes, Rhayader. T: 01597 811 343
- Neil's Wheels, Rhayader. T: 07495 919 508
- Elan Valley Visitor Centre & Bike Hub, Elan Village. T: 01597 810 880. Located at the Elan Valley visitor centre, there are bike washing facilities, a bike workshop, changing cubicles, toilets and a cafe on site.

L–R: Monks' Trod (Llwybr y Mynaich); river crossing in Cwm Egnant; bothy with a view; dinner in the sun; Lluest Cwmbach bothy.

10 MYNYDD EPYNT & THE DOETHIE VALLEY

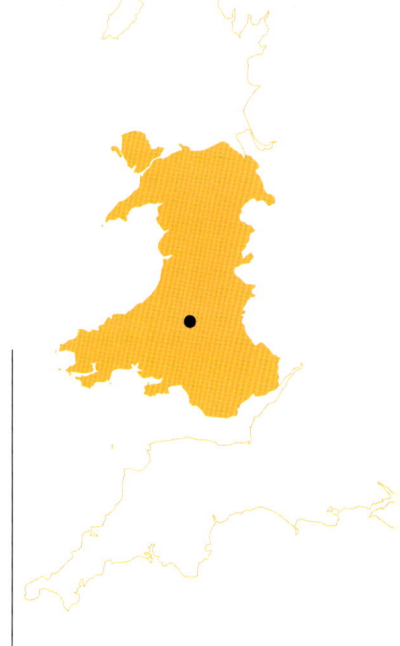

INTRODUCTION
Just south of Rhayader (Rhaeadr Gwy), the Cambrian Mountains slope down to meet the Irfon Valley and its historic spa towns. Builth Wells (Llanfair-ym-Muallt) is famous for its popular, annual Royal Welsh Show, while nearby Llanwrtyd Wells – Wales's smallest town – has reinvented itself as the host of various extreme and unusual events including the annual Man versus Horse race and the World Mountain Bike Bog Snorkelling Championships. Across the valley, the uplands of Mynydd Epynt are just as unusual; this huge moorland plateau is home to the Sennybridge Training Area (SENTA) and is kept off-limits to the public for much of the year by the military. However, there is a special permissive bridleway around its perimeter known as the Epynt Way, which offers some surprisingly good riding with views out to Pen y Fan.

ROUTE OVERVIEW
Tracing a rough circle around Llanwrtyd Wells, this route offers a challenging alternative for bikepackers wanting to sample more of Mid Wales beyond the Elan Valley and the Trans Cambrian Way. Starting in Builth Wells, the northern half of the route crosses the wild moorland of Abergwesyn Common before turning west towards the southern reaches of Elenydd and Mynydd Mallaen that are home to Llyn Brianne Reservoir, the Devil's Staircase and the sprawling Tywi Forest. The southern half of the route explores Mynydd Epynt, taking riders along its exposed escarpment on the waymarked Epynt Way, past SENTA's red warning flags, scattered bullet casings and nonchalant sheep. However, the highlight of the route is the almost-seven-kilometre-long descent down the

Classic Doethie Valley singletrack © RK.

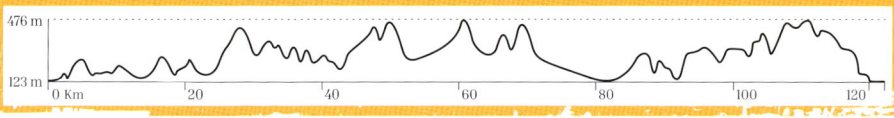

GRADE ▲ **DISTANCE** 122.4km/76.1 miles **ASCENT** 2,560m/8,400ft **TERRAIN** 70% off-road, with a mix of grassy bridleways and firm tracks, plus some technical singletrack in places **START/FINISH** Builth Wells **START/FINISH GRID REFERENCE** SO 042511 **BIKE-FRIENDLY PUBLIC TRANSPORT** Builth Road station, just north of Builth Wells **SATNAV** LD2 3DT **MAP** OS Explorer 187, Llandovery; 188, Builth Wells; 200, Llandrindod Wells & Elan Valley (1:25,000) **RECOMMENDED BIKE** Mountain bike

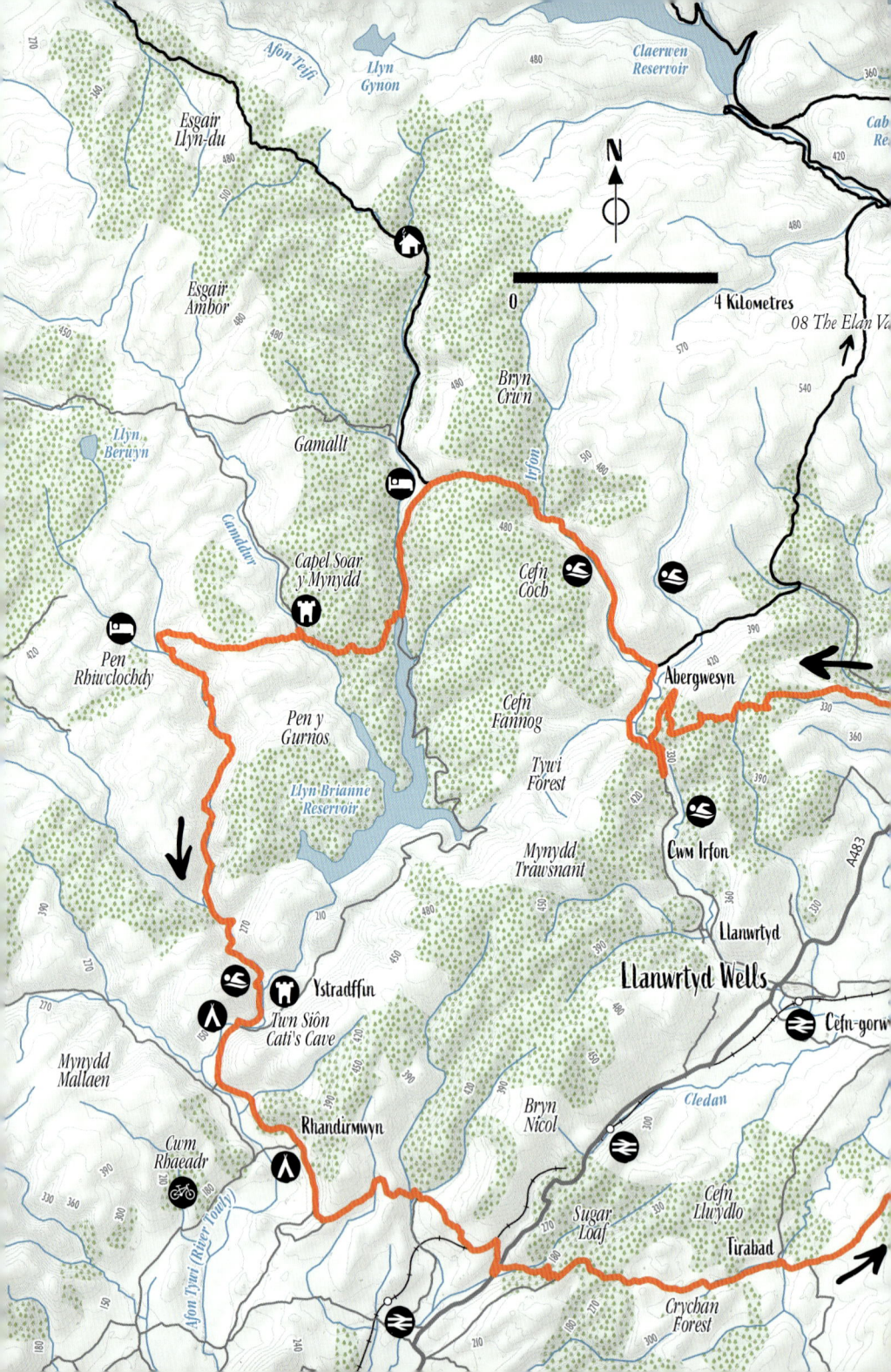

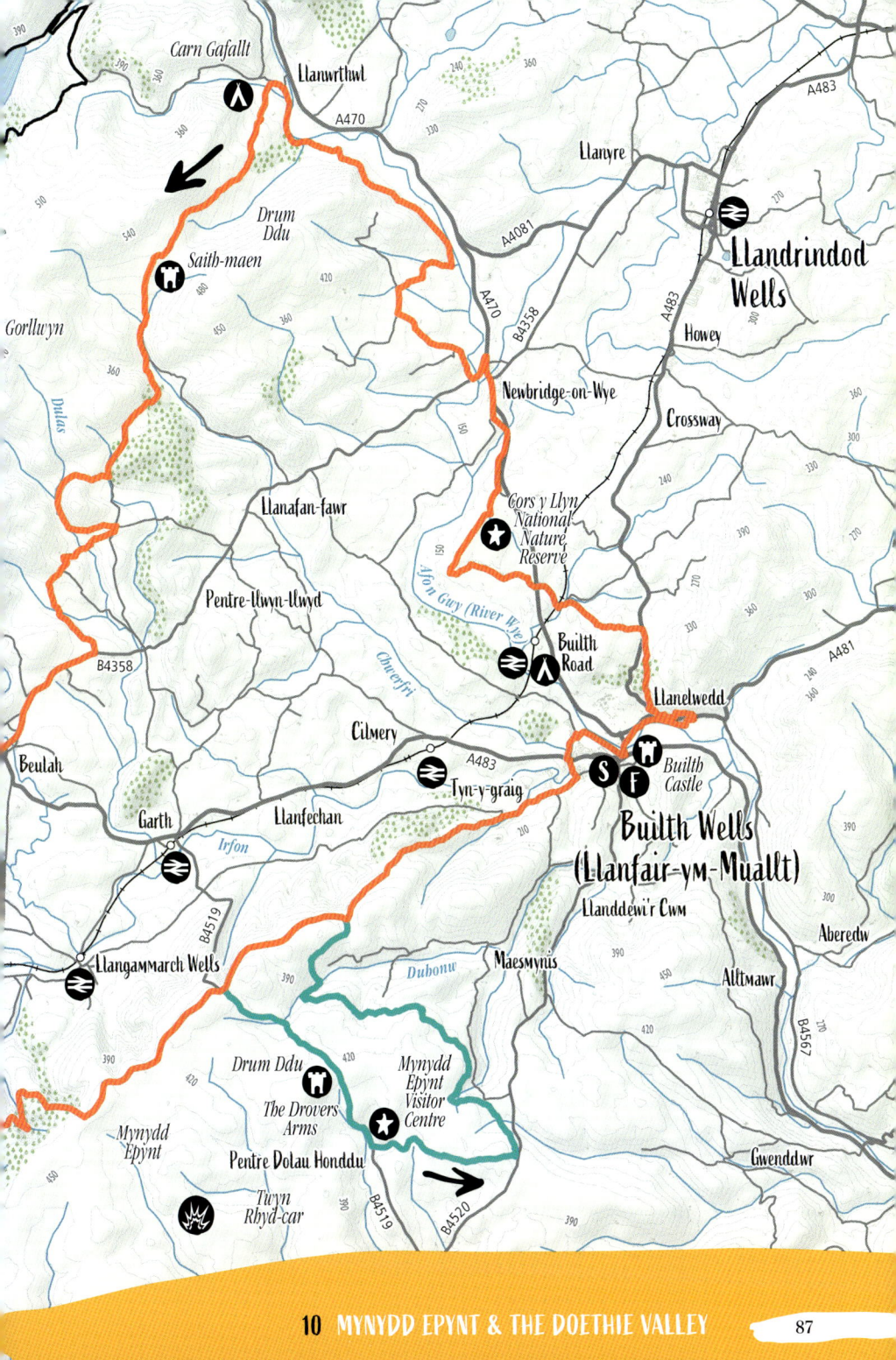

10 MYNYDD EPYNT & THE DOETHIE VALLEY   87

Doethie Valley – one of the longest and finest pieces of natural singletrack in the UK.

THE ROUTE

'There are many places in Wales of which I am fond, all of them entrancing in their different ways and at their proper seasons. But if I were asked by a stranger to this loveliest of all countries which place is the most beautiful, then I would tell of the pleasure in walking up the Afon Doethie on a fine day in the high spring of May or June when ... bluebells shimmer like a low flame amongst the woods.'   **Jim Perrin**, *Travels with the Flea* (2002)

Wales's ancient woodlands are often carpeted in thick swathes of purple come late spring, and Gwenffrwd-Dinas Nature Reserve at the southern end of the Doethie Valley is no exception. In May and early June, the shady forest floor under its gnarled oak trees becomes smothered in bluebells. The flowers love the rich, undisturbed soil in this long-established wood, but the area is also renowned for the bluebell displays on its open hillsides. These traditionally woodland flowers cover the slopes around Llyn Brianne, Abergwesyn and the Doethie Valley with a shimmering, blue-tinged haze. To reach these places requires a certain level of effort and commitment – all of these places are remote even by Welsh standards – which is where bikepacking here comes into its own. This overnight loop allows riders to penetrate right into the heart of this wild and relatively inaccessible corner of the Cambrian Mountains.

In contrast, this loop begins in Builth Wells. The busy market town is well-connected for Mid Wales, with nearby Builth Road railway station just off-route on the Heart of Wales Line. The route crosses the River Wye on the pretty Wye Bridge, passing the Royal Welsh Showground to hunt out some surprisingly good singletrack around the edge of Llanelwedd Quarries. A series of byways lead north to reach Newbridge-on-Wye before joining Sustrans Route 8 almost all the way to the Elan Valley. Just before reaching Rhayader, the route turns off the cycle path to begin the first sustained climb of the route up over Rhos Saith-maen ('Seven Stone Common') on a wide track through the high moorland.

NAVIGATION

The start of the Doethie Valley singletrack is easy to miss – look out for the bridleway sign and gate on your left before the bridge. The Epynt Way is clearly waymarked at regular intervals with yellow-topped wooden posts, as well as signs with a circular logo of a stylised white horse's head on a green circle. Although the Epynt Way is a designated route, it is not marked on OS maps: www.epyntway.org/maps

WHEN TO RIDE

The Doethie Valley singletrack is at its best in late spring and early summer, although there are a number of sections which never fully dry out. The singletrack also gets quite overgrown when the bracken grows high in June. The Epynt Way is particularly exposed with little shelter – there is a reason the military chose this area to test the mettle of their troops and recreate different fighting conditions. Builth Wells gets very busy in July during the annual four-day Royal Welsh Show.

L–R: *Gwenffrwd-Dinas Nature Reserve © RK; Epynt Way trail signs; a standard day in Llanwrtyd Wells; nearing the end of the Doethie Valley © RK; breakfast in Tywi Forest; Capel Soar y Mynydd.*

WARNINGS

The track from Soar y Mynydd to the start of the Doethie Valley is badly eroded – it is still rideable but look out for the deep gully down the centre of the track. The Heart of Wales Line Trail crosses the railway track just before Gilfach. The Epynt Way skirts the edge of SENTA and is open to riders all year round, even when the red flags are flying (indicating live firing on the range). There may be sudden loud noises such as light artillery, pyrotechnics and low-flying aircraft. Observe all military signs, avoid touching any objects on the ground and keep to the waymarked trail. If you are concerned, contact the continually manned operations room (T: 01874 635 599) for guidance.

WATER

There aren't many pubs and cafes on the route, but there are plenty of rivers and streams to fill up from.

FOOD AND DRINK

- The Trout Inn, Beulah.
  T: 01591 620 235
- Premier Store, Llanwrtyd Wells.
  T: 01591 610 266
- Towy Bridge Inn, Rhandirmwyn.
  T: 01550 760 370
- The Royal Oak Inn, Rhandirmwyn.
  T: 01550 760 201
- Drovers Rest, Llanwrtyd Wells.
  T: 01591 610 264

L–R: *The Epynt Way* © RK; *Capel Soar y Mynydd's interior; SENTA warning signs.*

On the south side of the common, the route passes through Beulah on its way to the Irfon Forest. There is a lot of off-piste singletrack to search out here and much of it features in the Llanwrtyd Wells annual 'Real Ale Wobble' mountain biking challenge, just one of the small town's many unusual events. There are some great swimming spots along the River Irfon too – the Washpool (Pwll Golchi) is a deep and wide section of the River Irfon where local farmers once washed their livestock on the way to market, while Wolf's Leap is a popular spot further up the valley.

Riding through tiny Abergwesyn, there isn't much to see any more other than a handful of houses, but this was once an important meeting point for drovers coming from the west. Three main droving routes converged here, and the Grouse Inn (now a private house) would have been kept busy feeding the drovers and reshoeing the cattle that passed through. The drovers that operated in this area were particularly entrepreneurial. They helped establish some of the first independent Welsh banks, including Banc yr Eidion Ddu ('Bank of the

Black Ox') in Llandovery which was set up by the drover David Jones in 1799. It was one of the most successful of the many droving banks and was eventually bought by Lloyds Bank in 1909; they kept the symbol of the ox for a number of years before swapping it for a black horse.

Towards the head of the Irfon Valley, the steep hairpin bends of the Devil's Staircase come into view. There's no getting away from the fact that this is a very challenging road climb, especially on a loaded bike. At the northern end of Llyn Brianne Reservoir, there is a more welcome surprise as you emerge from the Tywi Forest. The whitewashed walls of Capel Soar y Mynydd ('Zoar of the Mountains') appear out of nowhere in a clearing by the bridge. The chapel was built in 1822 to serve a scattered congregation of farmers from all over Elenydd. Inside, sunlight streams in through the high arched windows, a vase of wild flowers sits below the pulpit, and rows of angled, boxed pews face the altar under the words *Duw cariad yw* ('God is love'). A couple of miles further on and just off-route, Ty'n Cornel Hostel is another welcome refuge.

The start of the Doethie Valley singletrack is marked with a simple lichen-covered signpost before a footbridge. A small gate leads down to the head of the V-shaped valley, cloaked in vivid green bracken and cut through with a sliver of hard-baked dirt above the Afon Doethie. The ungroomed singletrack is classic old-school riding; it is stop–start in places with muddy sections, stream crossings and stretches of boggy ground to contend with, but when the trail finds its flow, it becomes an utter joy to ride. At times, the singletrack

ACCOMMODATION

- Court Farm Camping, Builth Road.
  T: 07973 624 216
- Doliago Farm Campsite, Llanwrthwl.
  T: 07870 537 179
- Moel Prysgau Bothy
  (Mountain Bothies Association)
  – www.mountainbothies.org.uk
- Dolgoch Hostel, Tregaron.
  T: 01440 730 226
- Ty'n Cornel Hostel, Tregaron.
  T: 01440 730 226
- Gelli Fechan Camping and Caravan
  Site, Rhandirmwyn. T: 07929 858 141
- Rhandirmwyn – Camping and
  Caravanning Club Site, Rhandirmwyn.
  T: 01550 760 257

Wild camping is not permitted on the Epynt Way as it goes through a military training area.

L–R: *The Drovers Arms © RK; start of the Doethie Valley singletrack © RK.*

is so good that it feels as if all the riding up until now – with its backdrop of remote chapels, old woodlands and native bluebells – has merely been a pretty distraction on the way to the main event. Few trails outside the Scottish Highlands come close to matching the wild and remote feeling you get riding here, and the singletrack maintains its quality the entire way down the valley, offering up one surprise after another. The trail also passes the RSPB's Gwenffrwd-Dinas Nature Reserve which is worth exploring on foot if you have the time – take the circular path around the wooded hill to seek out Twm Siôn Cati's cave – before following the Heart of Wales Line Trail east towards Mynydd Epynt.

The Sennybridge Training Area is one of the largest military training grounds in the UK and covers much of Mynydd Epynt ('Mountain Haunt of the Horses'). The land was requisitioned by the military in 1939 during World War II, which led to the controversial eviction of over 200 people and the loss of a predominantly Welsh-speaking community. In the distance, SENTA's skyline is dotted with small, rectangular conifer plantations that have been deliberately planted by the military to provide strategic markers, camouflage and cover for troops during exercises. They give the mountainous plateau a distinctive look and feel along with the red flags, abandoned

farm buildings, discarded smoke grenades and the occasional sound of gunfire. Public access is limited, but you can ride all the way around the perimeter of the training area on a permissive bridleway known as the Epynt Way, which is open even during live firing.

The route joins the northern section of the Epynt Way at Tirabad and climbs up through Crychan Forest to reach the Mabbions Way military road. It was first built in the 1940s, but its temptingly smooth tarmac looks like it could have been laid only yesterday. At the Garth Road viewpoint, there is the option to extend the route south past the Drovers Arms (now used by soldiers as an overnight shelter) to Disgwylfa Visitor Centre. From here, the eastern part of the Epynt Way follows a very faint, undulating path heading north on energy-sapping grass; it is wonderfully deserted but very challenging. The main route stays right on the escarpment edge instead, following one of the best sections on the Epynt Way as it drops down under the picnic benches to skirt high above Cwm Graig-ddu on narrow grassy singletrack. Follow the Epynt Way markers all the way to the edge of the military training area, before a fast descent leads back to Builth Wells.

OTHER ROUTES NEARBY

There is an excellent purpose-built mountain biking trail nearby at Cwm Rhaeadr, just north of Llandovery (Llanymddyfri). Llanwrtyd Wells hosts the annual Real Ale Wobble, a non-competitive mountain biking event which marks the beginning of the 10-day Mid Wales Beer Festival. The Coed Trallwm mountain bike trails are now closed to the public and are only available for guests staying in the on-site holiday cottages.

BIKE SHOPS AND HIRE

- Cycle-Tec, Builth Wells.
  T: 01982 554 682

NOTES

The Heart of Wales train line neatly bisects the loop, which opens up multiple route options.

11 SHROPSHIRE HILLS & THE KERRY RIDGEWAY

INTRODUCTION
The Shropshire Hills Area of Outstanding Natural Beauty lies just to the east of the border between England and Wales, stretching from the Clun Forest near Knighton (Tref-y-Clawdd) up to the Wrekin near Telford. Around the Long Mynd and the Stiperstones in particular, the steep hills contain a compact network of superb singletrack trails that disappear down narrow valleys locally known as 'batches'. The hills bridge the flat plains of the Marches and the grassy uplands of Mid Wales, and the Welsh influence is reflected in many place names just across the border ('mynydd' is Welsh for 'mountain'). The abundance of hillforts and castles, as well as Offa's Dyke – one of the longest linear earthworks in Britain – serves as a visual reminder of this area's turbulent history as a contested borderland.

ROUTE OVERVIEW
This tough, hilly but wonderfully remote-feeling loop joins together the varied trails on either side of the border. It heads into Wales on the start of the Trans Cambrian Way, using a series of grassy bridleways, quiet lanes and wind farm tracks to link up with the Kerry Ridgeway for almost 15 kilometres of glorious, high-level riding. Back across the border, the route squeezes in as much quality riding on the Stiperstones and the Long Mynd as possible, including the narrow ribbon of permissive singletrack around Nover's Hill and Jonathan's Hollow, before turning back to the border once more.

Permissive bridleway above Church Stretton, the Long Mynd © RK.

GRADE ▲ **DISTANCE** 130.8km/81.3 miles **ASCENT** 2,330m/7,644ft **TERRAIN** 70% off-road, mainly on non-technical grass-based bridleways and dirt tracks; some very steep climbs **START/FINISH** Knighton railway station **START/FINISH GRID REFERENCE** SO 290324 **BIKE-FRIENDLY PUBLIC TRANSPORT** At the start/finish **SATNAV** LD7 1DT **MAP** OS Explorer 201, Knighton & Presteigne; 214, Llanidloes & Newtown; 216, Welshpool & Montgomery; 217, The Long Mynd & Wenlock Edge (1:25,000) **RECOMMENDED BIKE** Mountain bike

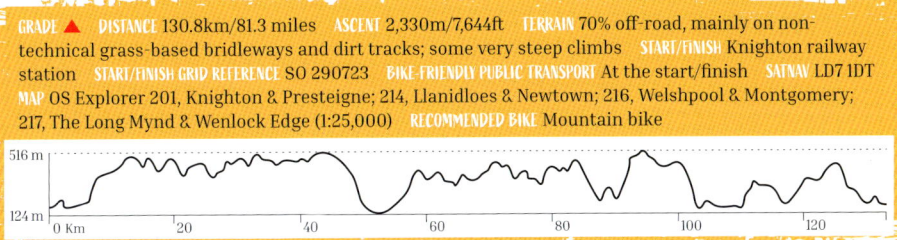

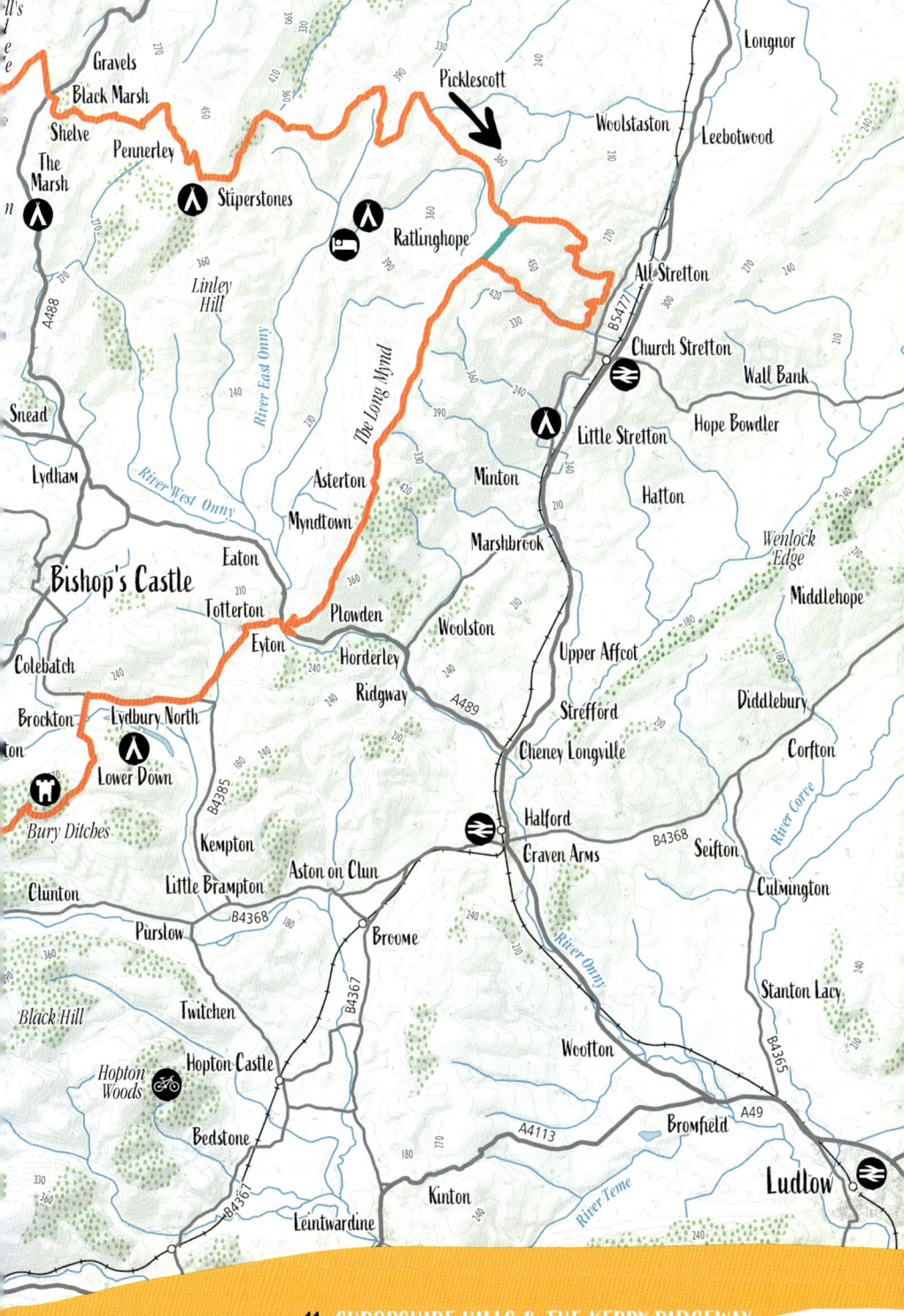

THE ROUTE

It is golden hour in early spring. The evening is clear and the bike lights remain in the saddle bag for now, but it is cold to still be out riding in the last of the day's light. Knighton isn't far though, just a steep descent away in the Teme Valley. A well-surfaced gravel track stays high on the ridgeline in front with a thin strip of grass running up its middle. The huge, rounded earthwork of Offa's Dyke runs parallel to the track, its shape somehow sharper and more defined in the low evening sun as it follows the contours of the hills into the distance.

The Shropshire Hills offer excellent riding, wonderful views and the greatest concentration of medieval castle earthworks anywhere in Britain, but their western edge is dominated by Offa's Dyke – Britain's longest monument and one of its most extraordinary. The enormous hand-dug bank and ditch runs north to south roughly along the modern border between England and Wales and was constructed in the late eighth century on the orders of the powerful Anglo-Saxon King of Mercia, Offa. The first mention of the dyke crops up in a biography of Alfred the Great, written around 100 years after Offa's death. A Welsh bishop named Asser wrote: 'There was ... an energetic king called Offa, terrifying to all the neighbouring kings and provinces around him, who ordered a great ditch to be made between Britain and Mercia.' Offa's Dyke faces west into modern-day Wales and was most likely built as both a cultural and political border and a visible display of power.

Around 130 kilometres of the dyke now survive in varying states of preservation. Walkers have been able to experience the huge earthwork close up on the Offa's Dyke Path since it was opened in 1971 as a National Trail, but there is no cycling equivalent. However, this route does finish along Llanfair Hill on a byway parallel to one of the best preserved and most continuous sections of the dyke. The track stays high above the Teme Valley, shadowing the monument's movements along the top of the hill for around three kilometres.

The route starts close by in Knighton, right on the border between England and Wales. The town's Welsh name, Tref-y-Clawdd, literally means 'Farm by the Dyke', and it is one of

NAVIGATION NOTES

The route follows part of the Jack Mytton Way which is well signed – look out for a blue horse and rider on a yellow disc, although colours are often badly faded. MTB Shropshire and the National Trust have produced a trail map of the Long Mynd with easy-to-follow waymarked routes that use a number system – you can find it online: www.nationaltrust.org.uk

WHEN TO RIDE

Many of these trails are grass or dirt based. Some hold up reasonably well in wet weather, but most will be nowhere near their best and can become easily eroded. There is very little shelter on the route; much of the riding is on open ridgeways. The Jack Mytton Way is popular with horse riders and can get badly churned up in places.

L–R: *Golden hour on Offa's Dyke* © RK; *Clun Castle ruins* © RK; *bridleway down The Batch on the Long Mynd* © RK; *the Stiperstones* © RK; *MTB sign on the Long Mynd; Mitchell's Fold stone circle.*

WARNINGS

The Stiperstones National Nature Reserve is grazed by cattle – avoid riding between cows and their calves. If cows are on the path, walk safely around them and do not attempt to move them. The route passes an active gliding club on the Long Mynd, and tackles some extremely steep climbs such as those out of Clun, Churchstoke and Lloyney. Offa's Dyke is a Scheduled Monument and a sensitive archaeological landscape – please avoid walking on it and consider donating to the Offa's Dyke Rescue Fund: www.justgiving.com/campaign/offasdyke

WATER

Carry what you need and fill up when you can – opportunities are limited.

FOOD AND DRINK

- The Court House, Churchstoke.
  T: 01588 620 605
- Co-op Food, Churchstoke.
  T: 01588 620 226
- The Bog Visitor Centre Cafe, The Bog (seasonal). T: 01743 792 484
- The Bridges, Bridges. T: 01588 650 360
- National Trust Cafe, Carding Mill Valley. T: 01694 725 000
- The Station, Marshbrook.
  T: 01694 781 208
- The White Horse Inn, Clun.
  T: 01588 640 305

only a few places where Offa's Dyke, Offa's Dyke National Trail and the modern border actually coincide. The town is also home to the Offa's Dyke Centre which is well worth a visit if it is open. Leaving Knighton, the route follows the start of the Trans Cambrian Way (page 65), climbing steeply above Lloyney to reach Goytre Hill. There is a convenient bench and picnic table midway up the slope, tucked away in a small, fenced-off field with views back towards the dyke. The trail stays high on close-cropped grass all the way to Pool Hill where it joins Glyndŵr's Way. A quick section on easy wind farm access tracks and country lanes follows, before a scenic climb on unfenced roads leads up to Cider House Farm and the start of the Kerry Ridgeway.

The Kerry Ridgeway is one of the oldest routes in Wales. It follows an important, high-level route that was once used by drovers to take their livestock to the lowland markets across the border in England. The ridgeway track passes two weathered Bronze Age burial mounds known as 'Two Tumps' and then runs almost dead straight for 15 kilometres, staying high on a mix of country lanes, gravel tracks, forestry roads and grassy bridleways. It is virtually all flat or gently downhill the whole way – a welcome break from the relentless ups and downs that characterise this route. The trail is lined with wild raspberries in the summer, and on a clear day there are panoramic views out to Bannau Brycheiniog (Brecon Beacons), Cadair Idris, the Rhinogydd and the Berwyn Hills.

West of Bishop's Castle, the route turns off the Kerry Ridgeway to descend into the Vale of Montgomery. The valley is flat and peaceful, and it is hard to picture the area as a troubled border or nearby Montgomery as a garrison town. The easy riding doesn't last long, though. Corndon Hill is one of the steepest ascents on the route, climbing steadily on quiet lanes out of Churchstoke (Yr Ystog) before a dead-end road cranks up the gradient to reach a gate and the strange sight of an American-style mailbox in the middle of nowhere. There is still more climbing to come, but the route follows a superb grassy

byway over the col between Lan Fawr and Corndon Hill, past ruined farm buildings and giant puffball mushrooms fruiting in the grass. There is a short reprieve as the route continues north to explore the prehistoric landscape around Stapely Common, where it passes right through the centre of Mitchell's Fold stone circle.

Heading east, the route turns its attention to the jagged hills of the Stiperstones, a small area often overlooked by riders, and then on to the Long Mynd. Its smooth, whaleback ridge has its own historic track known as the Portway, and just like the Kerry Ridgeway it provides some wonderfully relaxed, elevated riding. It also gives easy access to the Long Mynd's exceptional singletrack around Nover's Hill, Jinlye and Minton Batch. Many of these trails are permissive bridleways thanks to the work of MTB Shropshire and its partnership with the National Trust.

Further south, the route follows the Jack Mytton Way past Clun and its 11th-century border castle (free entry). The impressive ruins sit high on a natural rocky mound and are well worth a visit. There is one final climb to reach Llanfair Hill, before some easy last few kilometres alongside Offa's Dyke. Riding so close to it, it is hard not to draw comparisons with other great linear monuments in Britain. Visually, the earthwork is no Hadrian's Wall, but the dyke's size and visual impact on the hills over 1,200 years later is still pretty remarkable. However, a recent survey report commissioned by Cadw, Historic England and the National Trail unit found that less than nine per cent of the Scheduled Monument is in good condition, and concluded that the greatest threat to its continued survival is simply 'benign neglect'. It is a sad state of affairs for the largest and most complete purpose-built early medieval monument in Western Europe.

ACCOMMODATION
- Bryn Heulog B&B, Llanfair Waterdine. T: 01547 528 155
- Woodbatch Camping & Glamping, Bishop's Castle. T: 01588 630 141
- The Old School Campsite, Minsterley. T: 01588 650 351
- The Nipstone Campsite, The Bog. T: 01743 792 073
- YHA Bridges, Ratlinghope. T: 0345 260 2569
- Brow Farm Campsite, Ratlinghope. T: 01588 650 641
- Small Batch Campsite, Little Stretton. T: 01694 723 358
- Walcot Hall Campsite and Caravan Park, Lydbury North. T: 01588 680 254
- YHA Clun Mill, Clun. T: 0345 371 9112

OTHER ROUTES NEARBY
This route follows the start of the Trans Cambrian Way (page 65), as well as part of the Jack Mytton Way between Church Stretton and Llanfair Hill. The Humphrey Kynaston Way links to the Jack Mytton Way and could be used to extend the route further north.

BIKE SHOPS AND HIRE
- The Shropshire Hills Mountain Bike & Outdoor Pursuit Centre, Church Stretton. T: 01694 781 515

L–R: *Sunset from Llanfair Hill © RK; easy riding on the Portway, Long Mynd © RK; signage on the Kerry Ridgeway; sheltered bivvy spot.*

12 MACHYNLLETH & NANT YR ARIAN

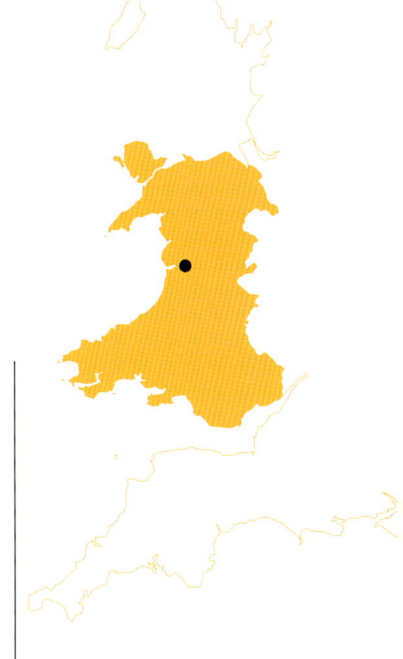

INTRODUCTION
The northern end of the Cambrian Mountains is dominated by the Pumlumon (Plynlimon) massif, a huge upland plateau lying in between the towns of Aberystwyth, Llanidloes and Machynlleth. This mountainous region is the highest point between Cadair Idris in southern Eryri (Snowdonia) and Pen y Fan in Bannau Brycheiniog (Brecon Beacons), as well as being the source of two major rivers – the Severn (Hafren) and Wye (Gwy). It is also one of the most ancient parts of Wales; the underlying rocks here are older than the Alps, the Andes and the Himalaya. At its fringes, the plateau dramatically gives way via steep cliffs, corries and scree slopes to Machynlleth, the Dyfi valley and the historic market town of Machynlleth – the site of Owain Glyndŵr's 15th-century Welsh Parliament.

ROUTE OVERVIEW
This fairly short but remote bikepacking loop takes riders up on the Pumlumon massif to explore the exposed doubletracks and rugged bridleways high above Machynlleth. There are no easy ways up on to the bleak and featureless plateau from the north – the route starts and finishes on some very steep sections – but the riding is fairly straightforward once up on the plateau and is suitable for gravel bikes. Navigation is also pretty simple as it uses the waymarked Mach 3 route (one of three great routes looked after by Beicio Mynydd Dyfi MTB), as well as linking up with some of the purpose-built trails at Bwlch Nant yr Arian on the way south towards Devil's Bridge (Pontarfynach). The return loop follows a wonderfully remote track past the eastern side of Nant-y-moch Reservoir. A technical descent known locally as 'The Chute' drops you back down into the Dyfi Valley to finish.

Singletrack at the end of 'The Chute' on Glyndŵr's Way.

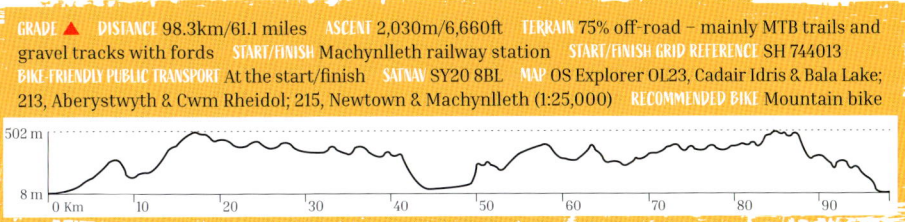

GRADE ▲ **DISTANCE** 98.3km/61.1 miles **ASCENT** 2,030m/6,660ft **TERRAIN** 75% off-road – mainly MTB trails and gravel tracks with fords **START/FINISH** Machynlleth railway station **START/FINISH GRID REFERENCE** SH 744013 **BIKE-FRIENDLY PUBLIC TRANSPORT** At the start/finish **SATNAV** SY20 8BL **MAP** OS Explorer OL23, Cadair Idris & Bala Lake; 213, Aberystwyth & Cwm Rheidol; 215, Newtown & Machynlleth (1:25,000) **RECOMMENDED BIKE** Mountain bike

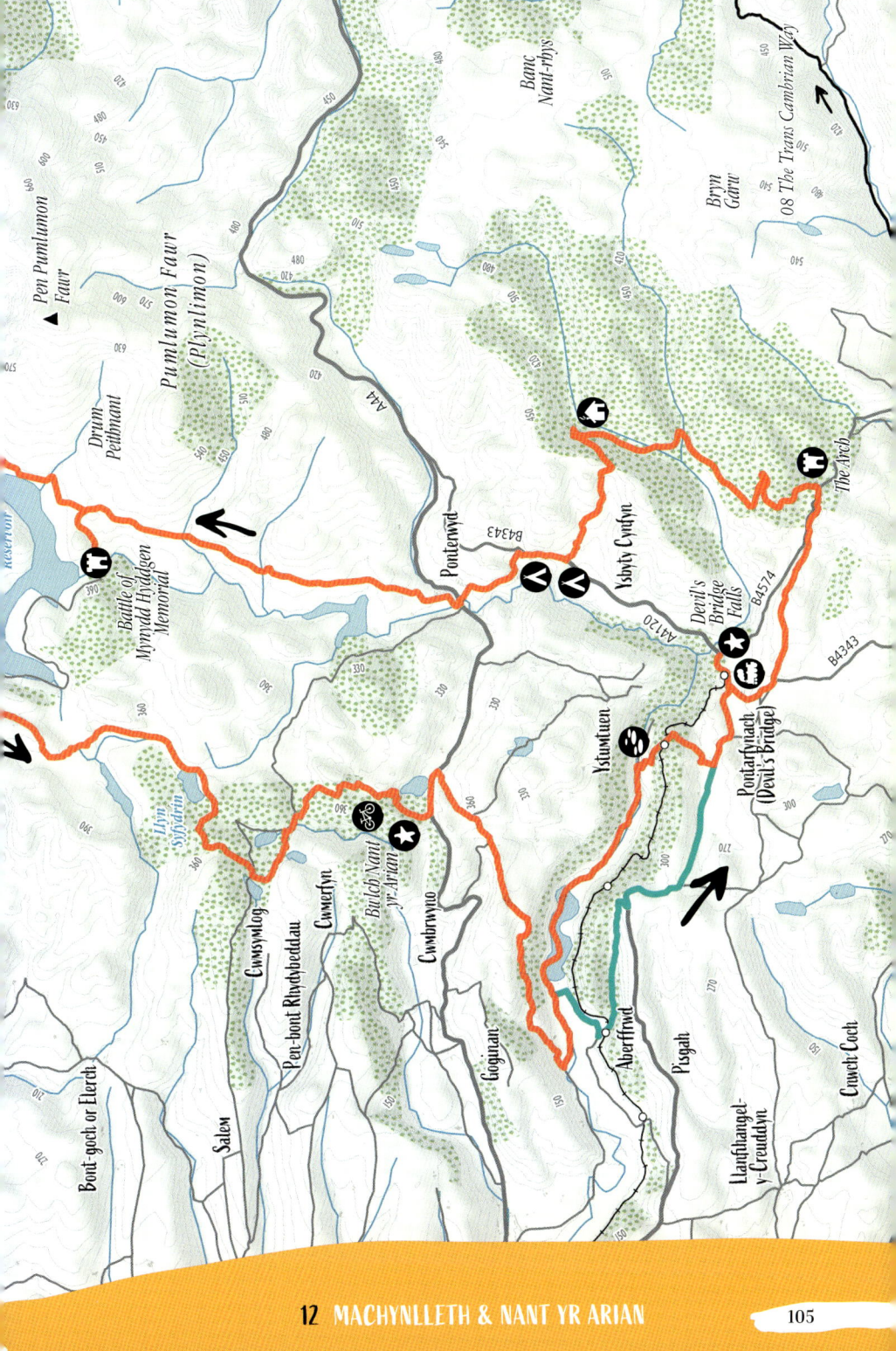

12 MACHYNLLETH & NANT YR ARIAN

105

THE ROUTE

Leaving the warmth of the visitor centre, the last of the late afternoon light has disappeared and the bike lights are on. Tomorrow is New Year's Eve and the road down from the pass is deserted. It's hard to judge speed or distance in the dark and the turn-off on the left comes much sooner than expected. Climbing up the track, a small beam of light projects out from the handlebars and scans the gravel a metre in front. It is silent except for the muffled sound of sheep tugging on the grass near the track. Every time the front light points towards one of them, two eyes glow back.

Starting at Machynlleth railway station, the route heads down the town's main high street – Heol Maengwyn – and past the Owain Glyndŵr Centre (free entry). It is well worth a visit to find out more about one of Wales's national heroes. Machynlleth is often called the 'ancient capital of Wales'; it was here that Owain Glyndŵr held his famous Welsh Parliament after being crowned Prince of Wales in 1404, almost 600 years before the opening of the modern Senedd Cymru (Welsh Parliament). Glyndŵr's vision of an independent Wales inspired many Welsh people to join his rebellion against English rule, and the uprising lasted for over a decade before he was eventually defeated.

The route follows the waymarked Mach trails out of Machynlleth, using a combination of quiet lanes and bridleways to reach the Afon Hengwm. The river soon narrows into a small, steep-sided gorge and the trail traverses high above the water on a ledge carved into the rock face. A prolonged climb on gravel tracks through the conifer plantations finally deposits riders on the edge of the Pumlumon massif, before the route continues south on a sunken and rutted roller coaster of a track under Foel fras. At Nant-y-moch Reservoir, the route joins the network of purpose-built and natural trails at Bwlch Nant yr Arian, including some of the Syfydrin Trail's most remote sections. The visitor centre's description of their flagship trail could equally describe this bikepacking route: 'it's the wild, desolate, lonely beauty of the far loops of this route that create its magic ... a unique mix of technical singletrack and ethereal

NAVIGATION

Navigation is fairly straightforward. The route follows some of the newly waymarked Mach 3 loop (www.dyfimountainbiking.org.uk) as well as some of the purpose-built trails at Bwlch Nant yr Arian.

WHEN TO RIDE

The route mainly uses rock-based tracks that hold up well in bad weather but there are a number of river crossings to contend with. As a bail-out option, you can take bikes on the steam trains of the Vale of Rheidol Railway that runs between Devil's Bridge and Aberystwyth, but ring ahead to reserve a space during peak times (T: 01970 625 819). The red kites at Nant yr Arian are fed daily at 2 p.m. in winter and 3 p.m. in summer.

L–R: *Red kite sculpture at Nant yr Arian Visitor Centre © Diane Kingston; The Arch, Hafod Estate © RK; remote track around Foel Fras © RK; Glyndŵr's Way; the Melindwr Trail, Nant yr Arian; signage for the 'Mach' trails.*

WARNINGS

The route joins a short section of the A4120 near Devil's Bridge, so take care. The forestry gate (grid reference: SN 768920) on the edge of Mynydd Bychan plantation is often locked so be prepared to lift your bike over. There are also some fords to be aware of: Afon Llechwedd-mawr (SN 751914) and Afon Hengwm (SN 783891) – both have footbridges nearby; the ford across the Afon Rheidol (SN 727781) is usually much deeper and there are access issue on the far side of the footbridge. You can easily miss this wide ford out and take the road back out of the Rheidol Valley instead (see the alternative route shown on the map and the accompanying GPX file).

WATER

There are numerous rivers to fill up from on the route.

L–R: *Warning sign at the top of 'The Chute'; ready for some night riding; golden hour in the Rheidol Valley © RK.*

emptiness, this genuine mountain route is one to savour, but certainly not one to underestimate'.

Just past Llyn Pendam, the route joins the Melindwr Trail on a wonderfully smooth and bermed switchback descent to Bwlch Nant yr Arian Visitor Centre. The cafe's balcony is an ideal place to watch the red kite feeding spectacle (free) at the lake nearby – these birds are unmistakeable with their reddish-brown bodies, huge wings and forked tails. You can expect to see as many as 150 birds coming in to feed, especially in the winter months. Bwlch Nant yr Arian became a red kite feeding station in 1999 and the visitor centre has played an important role in bringing these birds of prey back from the brink of extinction.

Past the visitor centre, the route continues south to the picturesque Rheidol Valley. A long descent on doubletrack leads down to a committing and wide ford across the Afon Rheidol; there is a footbridge nearby, but it is difficult to rejoin the byway on the other side of the valley. The route climbs steeply through Coed Rheidol National Nature Reserve on a mossy woodland trail and crosses the Vale of Rheidol Railway halfway up at Rhiwfron Halt. Time it right, and you'll see the historic narrow-gauge steam train puffing past the remote station on its journey between Devil's Bridge and Aberystwyth. At the top of the byway and a short distance along a road you'll find Devil's Bridge (Pontarfynach) and the Mynach Falls, one of Mid Wales's biggest tourist attractions. Despite the crowds, it is worth a short detour to see the three remarkable bridges that span the Afon Mynach – one built on top of the other – and explore its dramatic waterfall trails (£).

Soon after, the route enters the old Hafod Estate and passes through the iconic stone Arch. It was built by Hafod's most celebrated owner, Thomas Johnes, in 1810 to mark the Golden Jubilee of George III; the Arch is also a designated Dark Sky Discovery Site and has some excellent picnic benches. A maze

of forestry tracks leads down to Nant Syddion bothy as the route turns back north towards Nant-y-moch Reservoir.

On the eastern side of the reservoir, the route follows a dead-end road under Pen Pumlumon Fawr – the highest point between Eryri and Bannau Brycheiniog at 752 metres. The Victorian travel writer George Borrow wonderfully captures the wild, exposed landscape that unfurled beneath him from the summit in *Wild Wales* (1862):

> 'A mountainous wilderness extended on every side, a waste of russet-coloured hills, with here and there a black, craggy summit. No signs of life or cultivation were to be discovered, and the eye might search in vain for a grove or even a single tree.'

Not much has changed since Borrow walked here in 1854. The dead-end road soon turns into a glorious, rough gravel track that snakes its way up a remote valley along the Afon Hyddgen and past Bryn y Beddau ('Hill of Graves'). Tradition has it that this isolated area is the site of the Battle of Mynydd Hyddgen, a famous victory that marked a turning point for Owain Glyndŵr's rebellion in 1401. With the odds stacked against him, Glyndŵr's surprise success on the battlefield here meant that supporters began to flock to his cause – even Shakespeare referred to him as 'that great magician, damn'd Glendower', due to the Welshman's unique ability to infuriate the English Crown.

It is only at the edge of the plateau that you get a true sense of the height and scale of the Pumlumon massif. At Bwlch Hyddgen, the route rejoins the Mach 3 trail and skirts along the plateau edge on a wonderfully scenic and exposed bridleway. A sign by a gate warns about 'The Chute', just before the route plunges off the escarpment down a technical, rocky bridleway. Halfway down, the bridleway meets the Glyndŵr's Way National Trail and follows it almost the entire way back into Machynlleth.

FOOD AND DRINK
- Bwlch Nant yr Arian Visitor Centre Cafe, Ponterwyd. T: 01970 890 453
- Rheidol Filling Station, A44, Ponterwyd. T: 01970 890 649
- Hennighan's Top Shop Fish & Chips, Machynlleth. T: 01654 702 761

ACCOMMODATION
- Tyn Ffordd Fach Campsite, Ponterwyd. T: 07970 675 885
- Nant Syddion & Nant Rhys bothies (Mountain Bothies Association) – www.mountainbothies.org.uk

OTHER ROUTES NEARBY
Beicio Mynydd Dyfi MTB group is working with Natural Resources Wales to maintain and grow the trail network in the south Dyfi Valley, including the Climachx trail, which is just north of Machynlleth.
www.beiciomyndddyfi.org.uk

13 TOUR OF YR WYDDFA (SNOWDON)

INTRODUCTION

Eryri (Snowdonia) became Wales's first national park when it was created back in 1951. It is also the largest, providing a stunning backdrop of glacial valleys, forests, lakes, waterfalls, estuaries and beaches, but its nine mountain ranges are arguably what make it one of the most distinctive and spectacular landscapes in Britain. The biggest draw for many visitors is Yr Wyddfa (Snowdon), the highest peak in Wales at 1,085 metres. Just to the north, the rugged peaks of Glyder Fawr and Glyder Fach tower above the Ogwen Valley and offer views across to the Carneddau. The area is a stronghold of Welsh culture, language and identity – Carnedd Dafydd and Carnedd Llywelyn even bear the names of the princes of Welsh independence. Eryri is also renowned for its slate production which transformed the landscape here on a monumental scale; in 2021 The Slate Landscape of Northwest Wales was designated a UNESCO World Heritage Site.

ROUTE OVERVIEW

Riding up Yr Wyddfa has become a rite of passage for many mountain bikers. It's not every day that a bridleway goes all the way to a summit, let alone the summit of the highest mountain in the country. However, to get a sense of the true scale and grandeur of the mountain, this loop instead takes riders on a circumnavigation of the massif and the neighbouring Glyderau mountains. On the way, the route explores the area's industrial heritage at Dinorwig and Penrhyn quarries, passes two atmospheric castles built by Llywelyn the Great, cruises through the Ogwen Valley under the watchful gaze of Tryfan, and tackles the shoulder of Yr Wyddfa via its western slopes.

Previous page: *Ascending the Snowdon Ranger Path © RK. (route 13).*

Descending Yr Wyddfa via Maesgwm (Telegraph Valley) © RK.

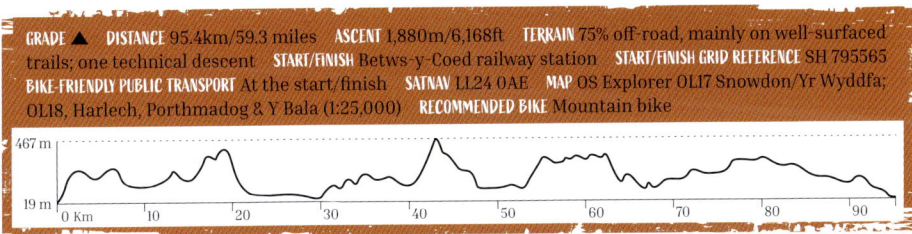

GRADE ▲ **DISTANCE** 95.4km/59.3 miles **ASCENT** 1,880m/6,168ft **TERRAIN** 75% off-road, mainly on well-surfaced trails; one technical descent **START/FINISH** Betws-y-Coed railway station **START/FINISH GRID REFERENCE** SH 795565 **BIKE-FRIENDLY PUBLIC TRANSPORT** At the start/finish **SATNAV** LL24 0AE **MAP** OS Explorer OL17 Snowdon/Yr Wyddfa; OL18, Harlech, Porthmadog & Y Bala (1:25,000) **RECOMMENDED BIKE** Mountain bike

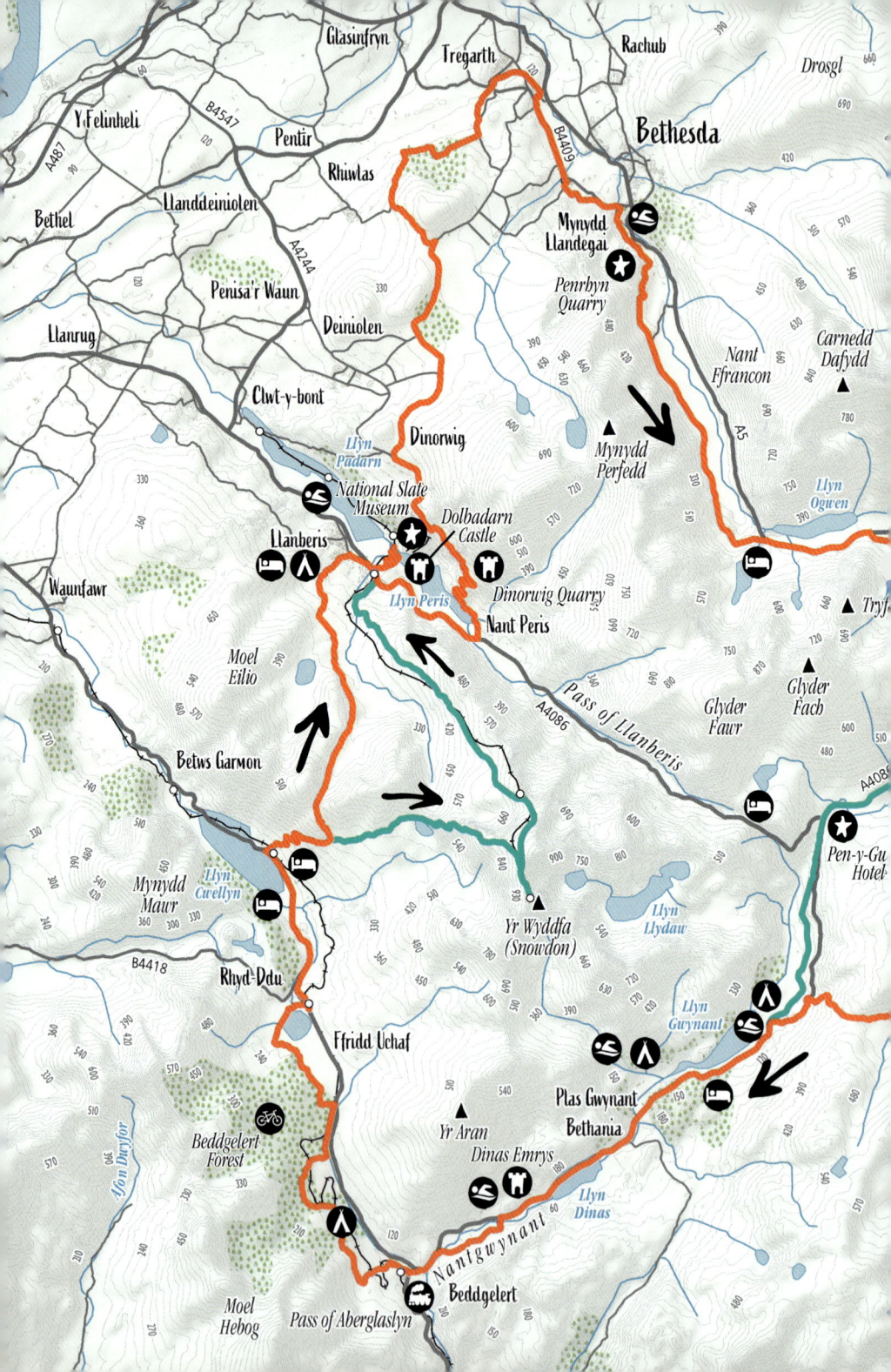

13 TOUR OF YR WYDDFA (SNOWDON) 115

BIKEPACKING WALES

L–R: *Riding beneath Tryfan* © *RK;*
Lôn Gwyrfai; Anglesey Barracks
(Dre Newydd) © *RK; Lôn Las Ogwen;*
Welsh Highland Railway © *RK.*

Despite recent resurfacing on some of Yr Wyddfa's bridleways, the route is still a challenging undertaking and racks up some serious elevation over its four major passes. The route also includes an optional, strenuous hike-a-bike ascent of Yr Wyddfa for riders keen to reach the summit.

THE ROUTE

Climbing steadily out of the Lledr Valley, the river and castle are quickly left behind. The few tourists wandering around its ruins have been shed too. Either side of the track, there is wool everywhere; white strands snagged on thick daubs of yellow lichen, soft wisps wrapped around fence wire and matted clumps blowing across the grass like tumbleweed. Crossing the high pass, Nant Gwynant suddenly opens up below and the overwhelming profile of the Yr Wyddfa massif rises out of the valley opposite, a wall of dark rock backlit in the afternoon sun.

Each of Eryri's nine mountain ranges are distinctive and unique. The Rhinogydd are renowned for their ruggedness, the Glyderau for their sea of sharp, angular rocks, and the Carneddau for their wild horses and stunning coastal location. To the south, the Moelwynion offer emptiness and solitude, while popular Cadair Idris provides a wealth of legends and unparalleled views out over the Mawddach Estuary. The jewel in Eryri's crown, though, is Yr Wyddfa. Standing 1,085 metres above sea level, the iconic peak rises higher than any other mountain in Wales; walkers, climbers and mountain bikers are drawn to it as if by some gigantic magnet, joining the many thousands of people that reach the summit each year. Despite this, the mountain still manages to maintain its aura of majesty and grandeur, even with its summit station and cafe perched on top.

Architecturally, Yr Wyddfa is undeniably magnificent. The late historian, author and travel writer Jan Morris called the peak a 'dream-view' in *The Matter of Wales* (1984), writing that it is 'exquisitely framed, its balance exact ... Cloud generally drifts obligingly around the crags of the mountain, and lies vaporously in its grey gulleys ... It is as though everything is refracted by the pale, moist quality of the air, so that we see the mountain through a lens, heightened or dramatized'.

NAVIGATION

Most of the trails are obvious on the ground, except for the grassy bridleway over Bwlch y Rhediad between Dolwyddelan and Llyn Gwynant which is wet, boggy and indistinct in places. The route also follows two clearly waymarked trails, Lôn Gwyrfai and Lôn Las Ogwen (part of Sustrans Route 82).

WHEN TO RIDE

The route passes through a mountainous environment which can be covered in snow throughout the winter and into spring. Check the mountain weather forecast before riding. Most of the route is on rocky tracks which hold up well in wet weather (Eryri is one of the wettest places in the UK) but there can be a risk of ice at higher altitudes.

The route uses the lower section of the Snowdon Ranger Path via Maesgwm (Telegraph Valley) to Llanberis and is accessible all year round with no restrictions. However, if you are considering the optional ascent of Yr Wyddfa (Snowdon), there is a voluntary agreement in place for cyclists which restricts usage of the bridleways to the summit between 1 May and 30 September. During these busy peak months, please avoid riding on these bridleways between 10 a.m. and 5 p.m. to minimise user conflict and help ensure that the trails remain open to cyclists in the future. www.mbwales.com/listings/snowdon

WARNINGS

The route has a few unavoidable sections on main roads, including short stretches on the A5 around Llyn Ogwen and the A4085 between Rhyd-Ddu and the Snowdon Ranger Path, as well as a longer but downhill stretch on the A498 to Beddgelert. The bridleway descent from Bwlch y Rhediad is very steep and technical – you will likely be pushing or carrying your bike down most of it. The route also crosses the Welsh Highland Railway line a number of times. The heritage railway can take bikes but check availability with the booking office before travelling (T: 01766 516 024).

OPTIONAL ROUTE

Yr Wyddfa (1,085 metres) is the highest peak in Wales and is a serious undertaking on foot or by bike. The Snowdon Ranger Path crosses challenging and exposed terrain on its way to the summit and is steep, loose and largely unrideable once past Bwlch Cwm Brwynog – be prepared for sections of sustained pushing and hike-a-bike. Carry a map and compass in case of low visibility as the bridleway passes close to sheer cliffs. Over 600,000 people hike up Yr Wyddfa every year and the summit can get very busy during the summer season. Please ride in control and at a speed that reflects your line of sight and abilities.

WATER

There are plenty of places to fill up en route. The Ogwen Centre at the Nant Ffrancon Pass also has public toilets and showers which are free and accessible 24/7.

This route takes riders on a sweeping loop around the base of the Yr Wyddfa massif to get a true sense of its size and shape, each high pass and deep valley offering up a new angle from which to view the mountain.

The route starts in Betws-y-Coed to the east of Yr Wyddfa and climbs steeply over the shoulder of Mynydd Cribau to reach the Lledr Valley. There is an easy stretch of riding along the river and under the impressive ruins of Dolwyddelan Castle before the route tackles its first high-level pass over the Moelwynion mountains. A wonderfully remote bridleway works its way up to Bwlch y Rhediad on a mix of stone tracks, boggy grass and brief slivers of singletrack, and then passes through a small, ornate gate standing in the middle of nowhere, its metal rusty with age.

Cresting the pass, you are suddenly confronted with the rocky bulk of the Yr Wyddfa massif for the first time. Gallt y Wenallt rises out of the valley opposite in an immense, forested pyramid of rock and scree. Behind it, a number of narrow ridges radiate out from Yr Wyddfa's summit, including Bwlch y Saethau ('Pass of the Arrows'). The impressive view can't quite distract from the largely unrideable, hike-a-bike descent into Nant Gwynant, although you can avoid this by taking the optional route on the main road from Betws-y-Coed instead, passing the historic Pen-y-Gwryd Hotel near the top of the Pen-y-Pass. The inn was used as the training base for Edmund

Hillary and Tenzing Norgay to help them prepare for the first successful ascent of Mount Everest in 1953, and is now filled with vintage mountaineering memorabilia.

The route picks up speed along the valley floor as it descends to the pretty village of Beddgelert. On the way it passes Llyn Gwynant and Llyn Dinas, which both offer idyllic campsites and swimming spots right under Yr Wyddfa's huge southern flanks. Riding here, it is easy to see how the peak would have been the ideal place for the Everest team to hone their mountaineering skills, especially in winter with Yr Wyddfa's awkward, rugged crags and razor-thin ridges coated in snow and ice. The mountain's English name comes from the Saxon word *Snaudune* – meaning 'Snow Hill' – while the Welsh name is linked to a local legend. Yr Wyddfa means a 'burial chamber' or 'grave', and the story goes that the giant Rhita Gawr was buried under a cairn of stones on the summit of the mountain after a battle with King Arthur.

Heading north, the route joins the Lôn Gwyrfai multi-user trail on an easy, scenic cruise through Beddgelert Forest under the watchful gaze of Moel Hebog ('Hill of the Falcon'). After emerging from the trees, the trail crosses over a wonderful, raised causeway along the edge of Llyn y Gader, before reaching the mining village of Rhyd-Ddu. Here, the route continues briefly on the main road running parallel with the Welsh Highland Railway – the UK's longest heritage railway – to reach

FOOD AND DRINK

- Caffi Gwynant, Bethania (seasonal). T: 01766 890 855
- Glaslyn Artisan Ice Cream & Pizza, Beddgelert. T: 01766 890 339
- Tanronnen Inn, Beddgelert. T: 01766 890 347
- Cwellyn Arms, Rhyd-Ddu. T: 01766 890 321
- Hafod Eryri Summit Cafe, Yr Wyddfa (Snowdon). T: 01286 870 223
- Pete's Eats, Llanberis. T: 01286 870 117
- Caban Cafe, Brynrefail. T: 01286 685 500
- Ogwen Snack Bar, Bethesda. T: 01248 600 683
- Moel Siabod Cafe, Capel Curig. T: 01690 720 429
- Pot Mêl Tearoom, Tŷ Hyll, Capel Curig. T: 01492 642 322

L–R: *Yr Wyddfa (Snowdon)* © RK; *Dinorwig Quarry* © RK.

ACCOMMODATION
- Llyn Gwynant Campsite, Nant Gwynant. T: 01766 890 302
- YHA Snowdon Bryn Gwynant. T: 0345 371 9108
- Hafod y Llan Campsite (National Trust), Nant Gwynant. T: 07929 662 770
- Beddgelert Campsite, Beddgelert. T: 01766 890 288
- Snowdon Base Camp Bunkhouse and Campsite, Rhyd-Ddu. T: 01766 890 321
- YHA Snowdon Ranger. T: 0345 371 9659
- Camping in Llanberis, Llanberis – www.campinginllanberis.com
- YHA Snowdon Llanberis. T: 0345 371 9645
- YHA Idwal Cottage. T: 0345 371 9744
- Gwern Gof Uchaf Campsite & Bunkhouse, Ogwen Valley. T: 01690 720 294
- Gwern Gof Isaf Campsite & Bunkhouse, Ogwen Valley.
- Bryn Tyrch Camping & Bunk Barn, Capel Curig. T: 01690 720 414
- YHA Snowdon Pen-y-Pass. T: 0345 371 9534

OTHER ROUTES NEARBY
Lôn Las Peris is a short waymarked trail along the shore of Llyn Padarn. Beddgelert Forest has two waymarked cycling trails – Derwen and Bedwen – which explore the northern end of the forest on forestry tracks.

the Snowdon Ranger path (Llwybr Cwellyn). The bridleway is named after John Morton, known as the Snowdon Ranger, a local who guided clients to the top of the mountain in the 19th century.

Crossing the railway line, the route works its way up the shoulder of Yr Wyddfa's western slopes on a series of recently surfaced zigzags. What used to be narrow singletrack is now a gravel track – understandable perhaps due to the mountain's popularity and certainly easier on a gravel bike, but a shame nonetheless. This corner of Yr Wyddfa is much less intimidating with its grassy slopes and lack of scree and rocks, but it is still a sustained climb to reach Bwlch Maesgwm, which marks the start of Telegraph Valley. After passing through a gate, the trail cuts down through the valley on a gloriously long, flat-out bridleway into Llanberis. This path has also been heavily sanitised, but it has been kept fairly narrow and the awkward drainage ditches that used to catch out unwary riders have all but disappeared.

Llanberis and the area immediately around it reveal a different side to Yr Wyddfa. Slate has been quarried in these mountains since Roman times, but during the Industrial Revolution the area became the world leader in the production and export of slate. Its lasting impact on the local communities, the landscape and the area's cultural heritage has finally been recognised – in 2021 The Slate Landscape of Northwest Wales became a UNESCO World Heritage Site. Once past the National

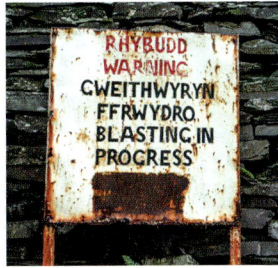

Slate Museum and Dolbadarn Castle (both free entry), the route climbs up through the magnificent Dinorwig Quarry and into an otherworldly landscape of steep inclines, huge, stepped galleries, deep pits and miles of cavernous underground workings. The entire mountainside has been consumed. Riding between the levels, though, the most compelling remains are those that offer a glimpse into the lives of the quarrymen that worked here. Just below the Dinorwig viewpoint, a steep path leads down to an old winding house with its rusted cables and drum still intact, while further down are the ruins of the Anglesey Barracks (Dre Newydd), built in the 1870s to house workers during the week.

Further north, the route joins Lôn Las Ogwen. The wonderfully scenic trail cuts right through Penrhyn Quarry on a narrow path that wiggles under vast spoil heaps of shattered slate, before climbing up to reach Nant Ffrancon Pass and the start of the Ogwen Valley. From here, the route follows a trail gradually down the valley through a spectacular mountain landscape, with the towering Glyderau and iconic Tryfan on one side and the Carneddau on the other. It is a particularly memorable stretch to end on. Once past Capel Curig, the route follows the Afon Llugwy back east towards Betws-y-Coed, passing the hugely popular Rhaeadr Ewynnol (Swallow Falls) (£) and over Pont-y-Pair Bridge ('Bridge of the Cauldron') to reach the station.

BIKE SHOPS AND HIRE
- Alpkit, Betws-y-Coed. T: 01690 507 307
- Beics Betws, Betws-y-Coed. T: 01690 710 766
- 1085 Adventures, Beddgelert. T: 07572 336 578
- Beiciau Greens Bikeshop, near Caernarfon. T: 01286 871 125
- The Bike Shed, Tan-Y-Bwlch. T: 07771 356 229
- Ebeics Eryri Cyf, Tregarth. T: 07877 822 592

NOTES
Eryri is pronounced 'eh-ruh-ree', while Yr Wyddfa is pronounced 'err with-va'.

L–R: *Nant Ffrancon Pass © RK; mistranslation in Penrhyn Quarry ('Warning - Workers Exploding'); Dinorwig Quarry © RK; Welsh slate.*

14 TOUR OF CADAIR IDRIS

INTRODUCTION
The mountainous landscape of southern Eryri (Snowdonia) is dominated by the distinctive shape of Cadair Idris (known locally as Cader Idris). The massif rises virtually straight from sea level to the summit peak of Penygadair at 893 metres and towers over the market town of Dolgellau to the north. The summit offers unrivalled views across the Mawddach estuary, over Barmouth's historic wooden trestle bridge and into the Rhinogydd (Rhinogs). The mountain's southern slopes drop down to the Dysynni Valley and the atmospheric ruins of Castell y Bere, a remote outpost built by Llywelyn the Great to protect his southern frontier and cattle herds. The valley is also home to the huge rocky outcrop known as Craig yr Aderyn (Birds' Rock) – the only inland breeding colony for cormorants in Wales – as well as a number of peaceful campsites and spectacular waterfalls at Dolgoch Falls and Nant Gwernol.

ROUTE OVERVIEW
Starting in the Victorian seaside resort of Barmouth (Y Bermo), this bikepacking route takes you across the Mawddach estuary to begin a tour around the Cadair Idris massif, with an optional and challenging out-and-back climb and hike-a-bike to the mountain's summit. Trail highlights include a scenic warm-up on the popular Mawddach Trail, crossing the shoulder of Cadair Idris on the prehistoric trackway known as Ffordd Ddu (the 'Black Way') and skirting high above the Afon Dysynni on some brilliantly narrow, exposed singletrack. While this route is fairly short, the Dysynni Valley makes the perfect overnight base to explore the quieter southern side of Cadair Idris.

NAVIGATION
Navigation is straightforward: the route uses several clearly waymarked trails such as the Mawddach Trail and Sustrans routes 8 and 82. The final steep descent from the car park at Ty-nant to the youth hostel is much less obvious – look out for the sporadic bridleway markers with a pale blue arrow on a yellow background. This bridleway is the most technical section of the route and is easily avoided by taking the road to the west instead.

Singletrack above the Afon Dysynni © RK.

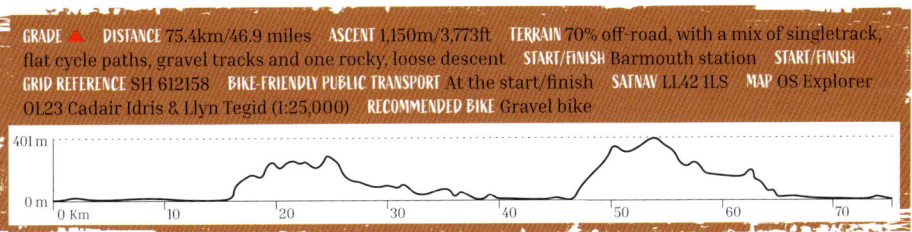

GRADE ▲ **DISTANCE** 75.4km/46.9 miles **ASCENT** 1,150m/3,773ft **TERRAIN** 70% off-road, with a mix of singletrack, flat cycle paths, gravel tracks and one rocky, loose descent **START/FINISH** Barmouth station **START/FINISH** **GRID REFERENCE** SH 612158 **BIKE-FRIENDLY PUBLIC TRANSPORT** At the start/finish **SATNAV** LL42 1LS **MAP** OS Explorer OL23 Cadair Idris & Llyn Tegid (1:25,000) **RECOMMENDED BIKE** Gravel bike

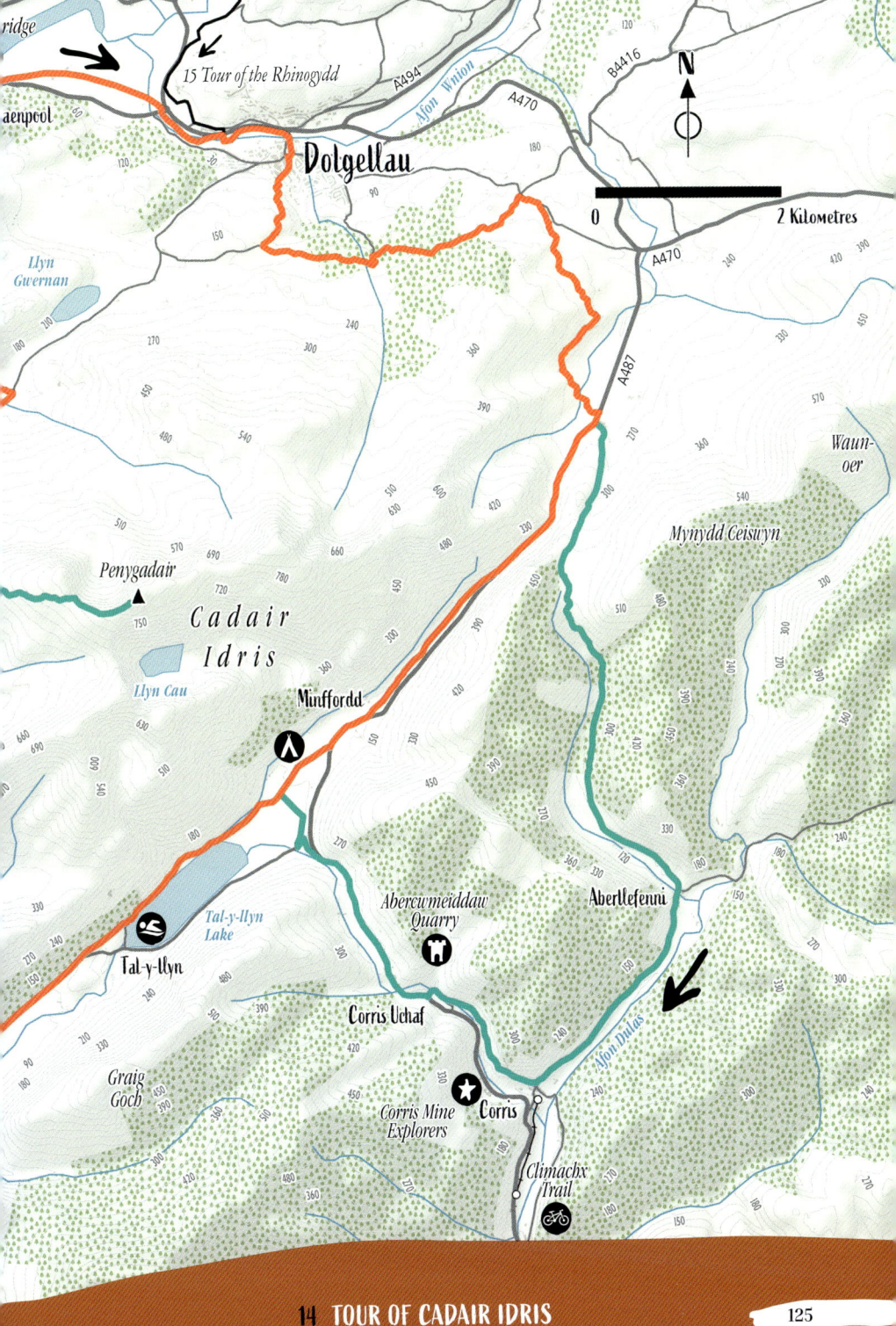

BIKEPACKING WALES

THE ROUTE

It's low tide at sunset and the estuary is turning orange. Ribbons of liquid gold carve meandering lines through the mud, the sun's reflections picking out each twist and turn as the water flows west. Across the estuary, Barmouth has been swallowed up by the darkness, while the wooden viaduct is silhouetted against the sun.

The ever-popular Cadair Idris only just makes it on to a list of Wales's 20 highest peaks, yet it attracts more attention from visitors than any other mountain in Eryri (Snowdonia) bar Yr Wyddfa (Snowdon). The mountain's appeal is obvious even from afar – the distinctive summit of Penygadair sits on top of a complex massif of craggy ridges, steep cliffs and hollowed-out cwms that are often filled with low-lying cloud, while its western slopes drop right down to the sea. The mountain is a superb viewpoint, with far-reaching views across the Mawddach Estuary and out over the blue-hazed curve of Cardigan Bay. Cadair Idris is also steeped in myths and legend. Its name is Welsh for 'Chair of Idris': according to local folklore Idris Gawr was a giant who was said to have used Llyn Cau near the summit as an enormous armchair. Penygadair means 'Top of the Chair', and legend tells that anyone who spends the night alone on its summit above the black lake will wake up either mad or a poet.

The route starts in Barmouth to the north-west of Cadair Idris. The mountain is a constant feature on the far side of the estuary, while on the hillside above Barmouth is Dinas Oleu ('Citadel of Light'), the first area of land donated to the National Trust in 1895. Rounding the harbour walls, the town's iconic viaduct comes into view, stretching across the wide mouth of the estuary between Barmouth and Morfa Mawddach and supported by hundreds of dainty-looking wooden posts. Opened in 1867, the Grade II listed bridge is one of the UK's longest and oldest timber viaducts. It makes for an exhilarating crossing above the water to reach the foothills of Cadair Idris.

On the southern side of the estuary, the route joins the spectacular Mawddach Trail (part of Sustrans Route 8) which runs right along the edge of the mudflats for almost 15 flat

WHEN TO RIDE

The surfaces hold up well all year round; much of the climbing is on tarmacked cycle trails and quiet roads, making it feel easier than it looks from the route profile. This route is ideal for a summer weekend, although Barmouth and its viaduct bridge both get very busy in the holidays. The popular Three Peaks Yacht Race starts in Barmouth and is usually held annually in June.

WARNINGS

There is a short, uphill section on the A487 to reach the start of the Bwlch Llyn Bach bridleway descent. The Blue Pool flooded quarry above Fairbourne is no longer accessible for swimming. The optional ascent of Cadair Idris (▲) is a huge climb but is surprisingly rideable in places: it starts off on a steep, grassy bridleway before joining the rock-strewn Pony Path and an unavoidable hike-a-bike on challenging and exposed terrain to reach the summit. Make sure that you carry a map and compass in case of low visibility as the bridleway passes close to sheer cliffs. There is a stone shelter on the summit but it is only intended to be used as an emergency refuge.

L–R: *Evening light over Barmouth* © RK; *descent from Tŷ Nant car park* © RK; *sunset over the Mawddach Estuary* © RK; *Barmouth Bridge* © RK; *Craig yr Aderyn (Birds' Rock)* © Steve Kingston.

WATER
There are plenty of streams and rivers en route to fill up from.

FOOD AND DRINK
· Ty Te Cadair Tea Room (Cadair Idris Visitor Centre), Minffordd.
T: 01654 761 505
· Ty'n y Cornel Hotel, Tal-y-llyn.
T: 01654 782 282
· George III, Penmaenpool.
T: 01341 422 525
Dolgellau has plenty of amenities. A number of the campsites en route also have small shops which sell local produce.

L–R: Barmouth Bridge © RK; fording the Afon Faw © RK; Abercwmeiddaw Quarry, Corris Uchaf © RK.

and scenic kilometres; this is a section of the disused railway line that once ran from Barmouth to Ruabon, near Wrexham. Unlike the mountains either side of the estuary, the valley floor is in constant flux – an ever-shifting scene of light, colours and textures as the tide ebbs and flows, exposing muddy gullies, saltmarsh, reed swamps and damp woodland teeming with wildlife. Rather wonderfully, the former signal box at the old station in Penmaenpool has been converted into an RSPB observation post.

The Mawddach Trail ends at Dolgellau, which once was a flourishing centre of trading and a hub of the woollen industry. The town sits at the very base of Cadair Idris, and as the route leaves the town, it climbs steeply up the mountain's lower slopes on a lovely little bridleway through avenues of birch trees and between high, moss-covered stone walls to reach the far side of the massif.

Passing through Bwlch Llyn Bach, the route descends into the upper Dysynni Valley. It feels much wilder and more remote compared with both the Mawddach and Dyfi valleys to the north and south. There are no large market towns or huge beach resorts to draw the crowds, instead the valley is full of spectacular natural features and some great riding.

At Abergynolwyn, the route joins a little-ridden bridleway above the Afon Dysynni on fantastically narrow singletrack through the bracken. The bridleway finishes near the atmospheric ruins of Castell y Bere (short detour; free entry), built in 1221 by Welsh ruler Llywelyn ap Iorwerth (Llywelyn the Great) to protect the southern border of Gwynedd and guard his cattle

pastures. The fortress sits on top of a wooded, rocky outcrop at the base of Cadair Idris; its extensive ruins are almost invisible from below, but a path corkscrews its way up through the woods to reveal a series of elaborate defences and views over the open valley. The optional route to the summit of Cadair Idris starts at Castell y Bere and joins the bridleway just after the hamlet of Llanfihangel-y-pennant. It is a huge climb that is not to be underestimated, especially as the bridleway starts only 55 metres above sea level.

Nearby, Craig yr Aderyn (Birds' Rock) is another impressive rocky outcrop that juts sharply out of the Dysynni Valley, rising to a height of 258 metres. It also has a steep footpath to the top and an Iron Age hillfort to explore – the path passes right through the original entrance to the fort. It takes its name from the abundance of bird life seen on and around its crags, including stonechats, barn owls, ravens, kestrels, red kites and nesting cormorants.

The route climbs out of the Dysynni Valley on a scenic, tarmac cycle path to join the prehistoric trackway known as the Ffordd Ddu ('the Black Way'); this is also Sustrans Route 82. As it rounds the shoulder of Cadair Idris, the Mawddach Estuary comes back into view – a vast, sprawling expanse of woodland, marsh and water that dominates the landscape below. A loose, rocky track leads down off the open slopes past a lone standing stone, before the route starts a final adrenaline-fuelled descent to reach the Mawddach Trail once more for an easy return to Barmouth.

ACCOMMODATION
- Dôl Einion Campsite, Tal-y-llyn.
  T: 01654 761 312
- Fferm Cedris Camping, Abergynolwyn.
  T: 01654 761 287
- Bird Rock Campsite, Llanllwyda.
  T: 01654 782 276
- Garthyfog Farm Camping, Arthog.
  T: 01341 250 254
- Cefn Coed Camping, Penmaenpool.
  T: 07398 630 571
- Graig Wen Camping, Arthog.
  T: 01341 250 482
- Hafod Dywyll Campsite, Islaw'r-dref.
  T: 01341 423 444
- YHA Kings, Islaw'r-dref. T: 0345 260 2761

OTHER ROUTES NEARBY
This route has been designed to link together with route 15 (page 131). Dyfi Bike Park and the Climachx trail are nearby too.

BIKE SHOPS AND HIRE
- Wheelism, Abergynolwyn.
  T: 07388 690 513
- Harbour Bike Hire, Barmouth.
  T: 01341 280 644

15 TOUR OF THE RHINOGYDD

INTRODUCTION
The Rhinogydd – often called the Rhinogs – in central Eryri (Snowdonia) dominate the landscape between Porthmadog and Barmouth (Y Bermo). The mountain range has a reputation for being one of the wildest places in the UK outside of Scotland. There are no tarmac roads over the mountains and exploring here can be tough going, with few paths, sharp rocks and deep heather to negotiate. Luckily, its southern end is much more welcoming, with a number of superb high-level trails to ride between Bontddu's gold mines and Harlech Castle (a UNESCO World Heritage Site). It's a magical place quite unlike anywhere else in the national park, home to an eclectic mix of coastal estuaries, dune systems, prehistoric monuments, ancient rainforests, huge waterfalls, a decommissioned nuclear power station and even the ruins of a small Roman amphitheatre.

ROUTE OVERVIEW
This clockwise route circumnavigates the rocky bulk of the Rhinogydd, passing through incredibly varied scenery and terrain as it switches between coast, forest, lake and mountain. An exhilarating ride along the Porthmadog embankment leads very steeply up and over to Llyn Trawsfynydd to link up with some of the world-class trails at Coed y Brenin. Once past Dolgellau, the route turns its attention to the Rhinogydd's southern slopes with a choice of two climbs to get you back to the coast: the atmospheric Bwlch y Rhiwgyr ('Pass of the Drovers') or the old Harlech to London coach road which crosses over Pont Scethin. Time it right, and you could finish with some optional beach riding too.

WHEN TO RIDE
The trail surface holds up fairly well all year round, especially the gravel singletrack around Trawsfynydd and the purpose-built trails at Coed y Brenin. The section over Bwlch y Rhiwgyr and the optional route over Pont Scethin cross high and exposed mountainous terrain and are best ridden in good weather.

Climbing up to Bwlch y Rhiwgyr © RK.

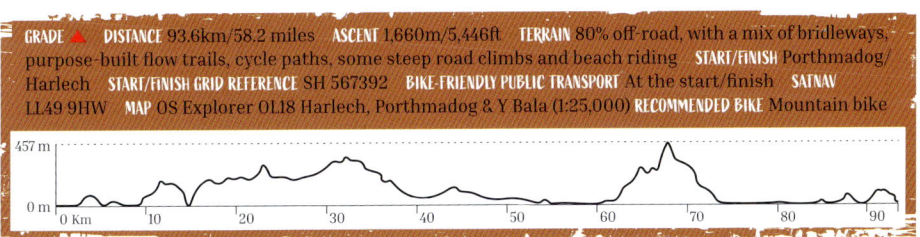

GRADE ▲ **DISTANCE** 93.6km/58.2 miles **ASCENT** 1,660m/5,446ft **TERRAIN** 80% off-road, with a mix of bridleways, purpose-built flow trails, cycle paths, some steep road climbs and beach riding **START/FINISH** Porthmadog/Harlech **START/FINISH GRID REFERENCE** SH 567392 **BIKE-FRIENDLY PUBLIC TRANSPORT** At the start/finish **SATNAV** LL49 9HW **MAP** OS Explorer OL18 Harlech, Porthmadog & Y Bala (1:25,000) **RECOMMENDED BIKE** Mountain bike

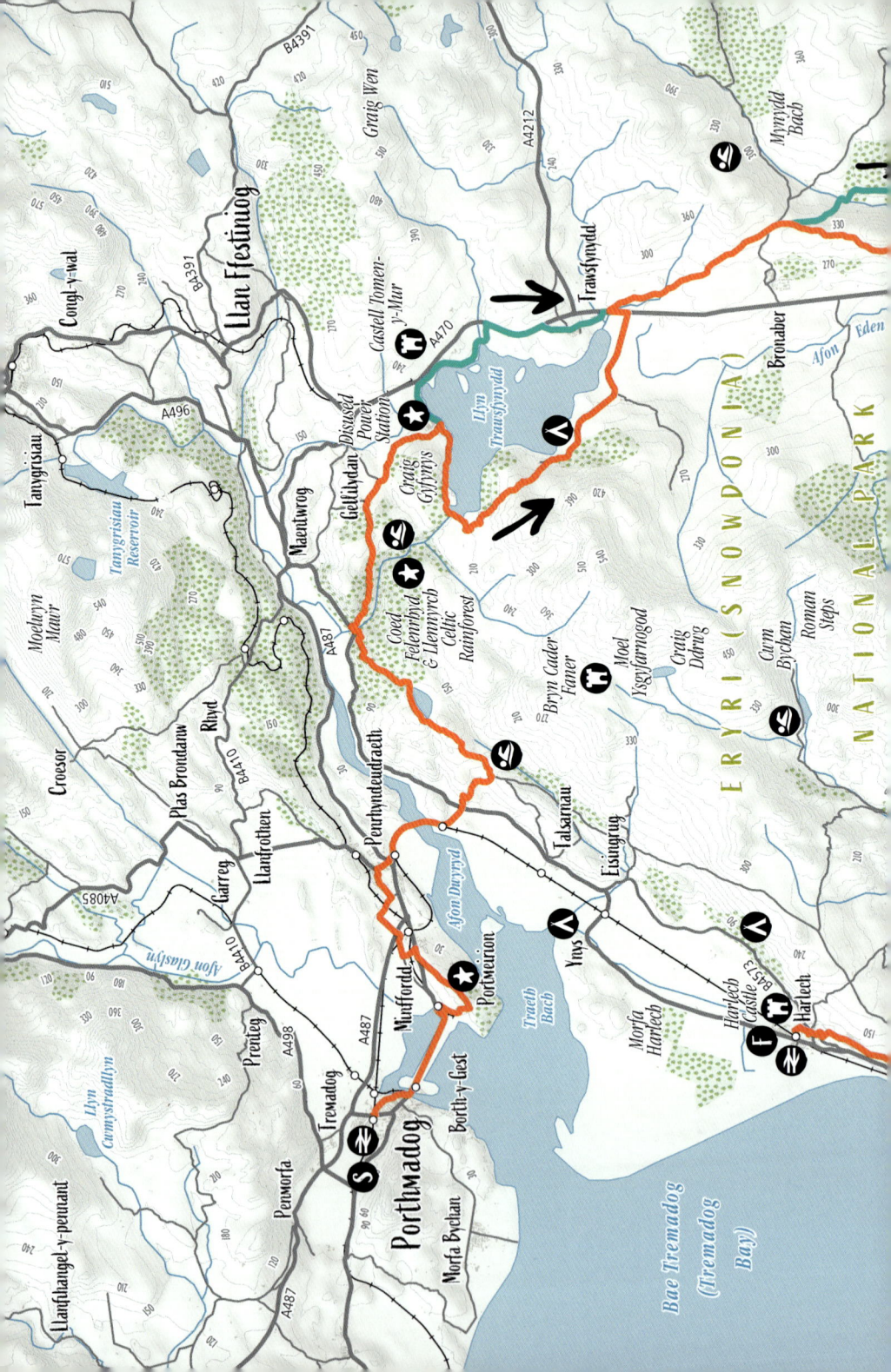

THE ROUTE

'These Rhinogs are part of the Snowdonia National Park. Does this mean that we can expect ice-cream shops, reconstructed footpaths and interesting leaflets? It does not. The bad-tempered Rhinogs are being left in their corner to sulk. There will be no car parks: get there at dawn for your two metres of muddy verge, or walk in from beyond some dismal bog. There will be no waymarks: in the Rhinogs you haven't really lived until you're lost. There will be no ice-cream.'   Ronald Turnbull, *Granite and Grit* (2009)

This bikepacking route around the Rhinogydd aims to show a different side to Eryri (Snowdonia) National Park. Some of the best riding on the route comes when you least expect it: the narrow lake-edge singletrack at Llyn Tecwyn Uchaf under the thrum of huge pylons, or the skinny gravel trails twisting in the shadows of Trawsfynydd's twin reactors. There is still enough unspoilt, big-mountain riding to give the route a suitably remote and rugged feel though. Even though the route never ventures that high, Eryri's huge peaks are a constant presence the entire way round: the Moelwynion range dominates the skyline to the north, with the Arenigau to the east, Cadair Idris across the Mawddach Estuary to the south and Yr Eifl on the Llŷn Peninsula to the west.

The route starts in the coastal town of Porthmadog, just outside the national park boundary. The town was once one of the great slate ports of Wales, exporting slate quarried from Blaenau Ffestiniog all over the world. The slate was transported from the mountain quarries on the Ffestiniog Railway (the world's oldest narrow-gauge railway) and the last mile of its journey would have been over the Cob. Built in the early 19th century by William Maddocks, this massive embankment was one of the most ambitious land reclamation projects in Wales, and it makes for a thrilling mile-long crossing over the old Glaslyn Estuary. There are superb panoramic views along the Cob into northern Eryri and on a clear day you can see Yr Wyddfa (Snowdon) lurking behind the rocky bulk of Moel Hebog.

After passing the colourful Italianate fantasy village of Portmeirion (£), the route tackles a savagely steep road climb

NAVIGATION

The route follows the waymarked Sustrans Route 8 over the Cob. The cycle paths around Llyn Trawsfynydd are well signposted. Coed y Brenin's purpose-built trails are clearly marked too, with large trail maps on the information boards in the car park.

WARNINGS

Just like route 04 (page 29), the section along Sarn Helen is rough and rocky, and gravel riders may want to stay on the Sustrans Route 82 instead which also ends up at Coed y Brenin's visitor centre. Bring change for Penmaenpool Toll Bridge and double-check opening times before travelling (bicycles cost 30p at the time of writing; advertised as open Monday to Saturday 8.30 a.m.–6.30 p.m. and Sunday 10 a.m.–6.30 p.m). Check the tide times before attempting the section on Morfa Dyffryn beach (Shell Island at the northern end is only accessible via a tidal causeway), otherwise stay on the road or use the train. Part of the beach is designated as an official naturist area and is clearly signed.

WATER

Amenities are very spread out, but there are plenty of streams and rivers to fill up from on the route.

L–R: *Llyn Trawsfynydd footbridge* © RK; *the Mawddach Estuary* © RK; *Sarn Helen Roman road* © Steve Kingston; *Harlech Castle* © RK; *low tide on Morfa Dyffryn beach* © RK.

FOOD AND DRINK

- Coed y Brenin Forest Park Visitor Centre Cafe. T: 01341 440 747
- Canolfan Prysor Centre Cafe, Llyn Trawsfynydd. T: 01766 540 780
- George III, Penmaenpool. T: 01341 422 525
- Caffi Castell, Harlech. T: 01766 780 200
- The Victoria Inn, Llanbedr. T: 01341 241 213
- The Ysgethin Inn, Tal-y-bont. T: 01341 247 578

The route also passes Dolgellau which has plenty of amenities.

ACCOMMODATION

- Cae Gwyn Farm campsite and camping barn, Bronaber. T: 01766 540 245
- Cae Adda camping and cabins, Llyn Trawsfynydd. T: 07783 873 532
- Merthyr Farm Campsite, Harlech. T: 01766 780 897
- Llech Camping, Ynys. T: 01766 781 082
- Bunkorama camping and bunkhouse, Barmouth. T: 07738 467 196
- Shell Island, Llanbedr. T: 01341 241 453
- Penrhos Isaf Bothy (Mountain Bothies Association)
  – www.mountainbothies.org.uk

OTHER ROUTES NEARBY

This route can easily be linked up with route 14 (page 123) around Cadair Idris.

BIKE SHOPS AND HIRE

- Beics Brenin, Coed y Brenin. T: 01341 440 728
- Harbour Bike Hire, Barmouth. T: 01341 280 644
- Snowdonia Cycles, Llanbedr. T: 07449 950 392

L–R: *Descent from Pont Fadog* © Steve Kingston; *swimming at Rhaeadr Du (the Black Waterfalls); singletrack around Llyn Tecwyn Uchaf reservoir.*

up to Llyn Tecwyn Uchaf reservoir. It hugs the edge of the water on wonderfully narrow and elevated singletrack all the way to the far end of the reservoir, ignoring the giant pylons, before descending on a cobbled track through Coed Felenrhyd and Llennyrch. This ancient oak woodland is a type of temperate rainforest – warm, damp and dense with mossy green rocks, lush ferns and rare lichens. The woodland is cut through by the Afon Prysor, which flows through a deep gorge and over dramatic waterfalls. Look out for Ivy Bridge by the main road, which would have been part of the old packhorse route from Harlech to Maentwrog. Only a short walk up the river, the magical medieval bridge is dripping in vines and almost completely coated in moss.

Heading south, the route reaches the edge of Llyn Trawsfynydd reservoir. This is Wales's second largest lake, after Llyn Tegid (Bala), but it is far from natural. The dam was originally built in 1922 to store water for the Maentwrog hydroelectric power station, before being raised in the 1960s during the construction of the Trawsfynydd nuclear power station. The nuclear power station was closed in 1991, but the long decommissioning process is ongoing and the area is still dominated by its two huge, square reactors at the northern end of the lake. As the route passes under the reactors, it joins a cycle path around the lake and you have a choice to make: the trail on the western side is more interesting and has better views, while the eastern trail is much flatter and has a brief but wonderful section of skinny singletrack right by the water.

Trawsfynydd literally means 'across mountains'. As the route continues south and cuts through the craggy, mountainous landscape on the Sarn Helen Roman road, it is easy to see why. It follows a gloriously scenic track across open hillside before

entering Coed y Brenin Forest, the site of Britain's first purpose-built mountain biking centre. This is where it all started. The first hand-built trails – including Tarw Du, originally called the Red Bull trail – were the brainchild of local Welshman Dafydd Davis who was working as a ranger for the Forestry Commission back in the 1990s. Coed y Brenin's success soon kick-started a trail centre revolution throughout Wales and the UK, and the forest now boasts eight mountain biking trails. This route follows the popular MinorTaur trail out of the visitor centre car park on twisting, flowy singletrack past two huge waterfalls, disused gold mines and abandoned gunpowder works.

Near Dolgellau, the route briefly joins the scenic Mawddach Trail along the estuary and under the foothills of Cadair Idris. A steep road climb leads up into the mountains high above Bontddu before the route traverses the southern slopes of the Rhinogydd on a fantastically elevated trail. Its surface alternates between compact singletrack, stone slabs and loose rocks as it skirts around ruined farmsteads to reach a series of technical switchbacks up to Bwlch y Rhiwgyr ('Pass of the Drovers'). At the pass, the trail goes through a clear notch in the ridge. It is an impressively atmospheric place, and it is easy to imagine the drovers and their livestock passing through here at the start of their long journey from the coastal plains around Harlech and Tal-y-bont to markets as far away as London.

The route continues on the old drove road on the northern side of the pass, racing down the grassy western slopes of the Rhinogydd towards the coast and past Lletty Lloegr cottage (the 'English shelter'). This building would have been used as an overnight stopping place for the drovers before they tackled the remote pass. Further down, the route crosses Pont Fadog and passes a telltale group of Scots pines nearby which were used by drovers to guide them to a favourite inn or a safe river crossing. The optional higher-level crossing follows the rather astonishing route of the old London to Harlech coach road which crosses Pont Scethin, a wonderfully remote 18th-century packhorse bridge in the upper reaches of Cwm Ysgethin.

The final section of the route closely follows the Cambrian Coast Railway, making it easy to adapt or shorten if necessary. If the tide is low enough, follow the main route north on the hard sand along Morfa Dyffryn beach towards Harlech Castle (£). Dating from the late 13th century, it forms part of an imposing chain of medieval fortresses built by Edward I to secure his land in North Wales, along with the coastal castles at Conwy, Caernarfon and Beaumaris. If the tide times aren't quite right, either take the train or follow Sustrans Route 8 on minor roads to Harlech instead.

16 CONWY & THE CARNEDDAU

INTRODUCTION
The north-eastern corner of Eryri (Snowdonia) is dominated by the Carneddau range. Bordered by the Irish Sea to the north and Afon Conwy to the east, it is the largest uninterrupted area of upland in the national park. These heather-clad mountains plunge down to the coast between Bangor and Conwy Castle, one of the best-preserved medieval fortresses in Europe. On the other side of the Conwy Estuary lies the Victorian seaside resort of Llandudno, as well as the Great Orme (Y Gogarth) which juts out into the ocean towards Anglesey (Ynys Môn). This spectacular limestone headland is named after the old Norse word for sea serpent and is home to a herd of wild Kashmir goats, the UK's only surviving cable-operated street tramway and the famous Great Orme copper mines – the largest prehistoric mines in the world.

ROUTE OVERVIEW
This fairly short and non-technical route explores the northern end of the Carneddau, with its wild horses, purple heather and golden beaches. Starting in Colwyn Bay, it heads west towards Llandudno to join the outrageously scenic Marine Drive around the Great Orme, before crossing the Afon Conwy and passing under the town's impressive castle walls. The second half of the route leaves the sand and tarmac to head into the mountains via the Sychnant Pass (Bwlch Sychnant). The return leg follows the remote Roman road over Bwlch y Ddeufaen, before dropping back down into the Conwy Valley.

Marine Drive around the Great Orme © RK.

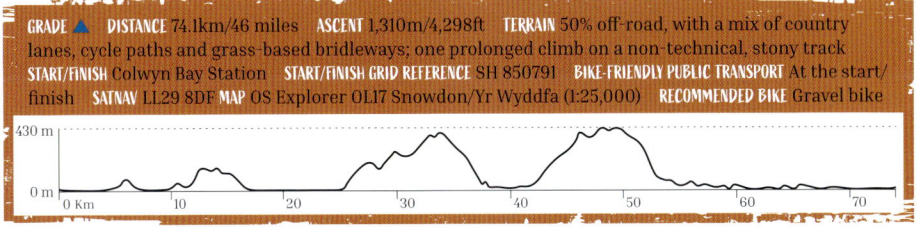

GRADE ▲ **DISTANCE** 74.1km/46 miles **ASCENT** 1,310m/4,298ft **TERRAIN** 50% off-road, with a mix of country lanes, cycle paths and grass-based bridleways; one prolonged climb on a non-technical, stony track **START/FINISH** Colwyn Bay Station **START/FINISH GRID REFERENCE** SH 850791 **BIKE-FRIENDLY PUBLIC TRANSPORT** At the start/finish **SATNAV** LL29 8DF **MAP** OS Explorer OL17 Snowdon/Yr Wyddfa (1:25,000) **RECOMMENDED BIKE** Gravel bike

16 CONWY & THE CARNEDDAU

THE ROUTE

'I walked nearly the length of The Parade, enjoying the chill … air and the trim handsomeness of the setting: a soft glow of hotels to the left, an inky void of restless sea to my right and a scattered twinkling of lights on the near and far headlands of Great and Little Ormes.'   Bill Bryson, *Notes from a Small Island* (1995)

Known as the 'Queen of Welsh resorts', the elegant seaside town of Llandudno lies between the headlands of Great Orme and Little Orme. It is a proper British seaside resort with a Victorian pier (the longest in Wales), traditional Punch and Judy shows, ice cream parlours, retro arcade games and donkey rides on the beach. The wide Victorian promenade – The Parade – follows the sweeping crescent of Llandudno Bay for almost two miles along the seafront and is lined with a string of handsome hotels painted in pastel colours, each with huge bay windows looking out across the ocean.

The route starts just to the east of Llandudno at Colwyn Bay station and passes through the holiday resort on a cycle path right by the beach. Once past the Little Orme, the rocky bulk of the Great Orme is unmistakeable in the distance – it juts out into the Irish Sea for two miles, rising like a dragon's head out of the sea.

At Llandudno pier, the route joins the fantastically positioned Marine Drive around the headland on a one-way toll road cut into the steep limestone cliffs. The narrow road was built in 1878 for horses and carriages at the height of Llandudno's Victorian splendour and is free for cyclists. Before Marine Drive was constructed, there was a dangerous footpath known as Cust's Path that followed a similar line around the headland. Although the road is much safer than the original path, Marine Drive still gives you a sense of exposure and vertigo as it clings to the edge of the headland. Follow it around the coast past herds of wild Kashmir goats and under warped and folded layers of limestone to reach West Shore beach.

The Victorians may have come for the bathing, fresh air and seaside hotels, but the Great Orme and the nearby mountains contain evidence of human activity dating back

NAVIGATION

The coastal sections of the route follow the waymarked Sustrans Route 5 around most of the Great Orme headland on a combination of tarmac cycle paths, quiet lanes and gravel riding right by the beach. Inland, the area's bridleways are well signposted and intermittently follow the North Wales Path between Conwy and Llanfairfechan.

WHEN TO RIDE

This coastal route is at its best in August when the hills are carpeted in purple heather. The high-level bridleway between the Sychnant Pass and Llanfairfechan is predominantly grass based and doesn't hold up well after rain.

WARNINGS

Cycling isn't permitted on The Parade along Llandudno seafront. The byway up to the Sychnant Pass becomes a tarmacked private road marked as a footpath for the final 200 metres – it is regularly used by local cyclists but walk this section to stay legal. The trail becomes very boggy before crossing Afon Gyrach (SH 740754) near Ty'n-y-ffrith farm.

L–R: *Druid's Circle (Meini Hirion); Conwy Castle and Conwy Suspension Bridge; Conwy Mountain (Mynydd y Dref); Druid's Circle; byway to the Sychnant Pass.*

WATER
There are limited places to fill up en route between Conwy and Llanfairfechan. Best to carry what you need.

FOOD AND DRINK
- Parisella's Cafeteria, Llandudno.
  T: 01492 592 448
- Rest and Be Thankful, Marine Drive.
  T: 01492 870 004
- West Shore Beach Cafe, Llandudno.
  T: 01492 872 958
- Co-op, Llanfairfechan.
  T: 01248 689 199
- Alma's Café, Abergwyngregyn.
  T: 01248 680 881

Llandudno Junction and Conwy offer further amenities.

ACCOMMODATION
- YHA Conwy. T: 0345 371 9732
- Platt's Farm Campsite & Bunkhouse, Llanfairfechan. T: 01248 680 105
- Cefn Cae Campsite, Rowen.
  T: 01492 650 011
- YHA Rowen. T: 0345 371 9038

thousands of years. The Great Orme copper mines (£) are thought to be the largest prehistoric mines in the world, and during the Bronze Age the site would have echoed with the noise of mining on an industrial scale. These early miners were digging for copper – an essential ingredient in making bronze – and left behind a vast complex of tunnels and passages. On the far side of the Conwy Estuary, Graig Lwyd was also home to one of the largest Neolithic axe factories known in Wales before modern-day quarrying destroyed the site.

Heading west, the route crosses over the estuary on Thomas Telford's suspension bridge and passes right under the walls of Conwy Castle (£). Conwy is the most complete walled town in Britain and is protected by an unbroken ring of thick stone battlements over a kilometre long. You can walk around the walls for free, high above the harbour and the maze of old streets. Its castle still towers over the town after 700 years and, up close, the stones still have traces of lime render on them – a faint reminder that the forbidding medieval fortress would have originally been painted white.

Past the town walls, the route turns its attention to the northern slopes of the Carneddau. The mountains in this corner of Eryri (Snowdonia) may not be as tall as the Yr Wyddfa (Snowdon) massif or rugged like the Glyderau to the south, but their unique position right on the coast makes them a spectacular place to ride. As the route works its way up over Conwy Mountain (Mynydd y Dref) to reach the Sychnant Pass, it emerges from an enclosed byway to be met with a riot of

colour; in late summer, the mountains here are transformed under a carpet of purple heather against a backdrop of vivid greens and blues.

Further west, the route joins a grassy bridleway over Penmaenmawr ('Head of the Great Stone') which is scattered with prehistoric remains. Druid's Circle (Meini Hirion) is one of the finest stone circles in the area – it's a very brief detour off-route, perched up on the flanks of Cefn Coch. From here, an exhilarating bridleway descends off the mountain on the North Wales Path, racing over short-cropped grass towards Nant-y-felin and the sea.

After a short stretch on quiet roads along the coast, the route cuts back inland to begin a steep climb over Bwlch y Ddeufaen ('Pass of the Two Stones'). At Abergwyngregyn, it passes the entrance to Aber Falls (Rhaeadr-fawr), one of Eryri's most dramatic waterfalls, before joining an old Roman road over the pass. The track once linked the Roman forts at Caerhun (Canovium) and Caernarfon (Segontium) and would have also more recently been used as a drove road to transport black cattle from the rich grazing lands of Anglesey and across North Wales to the east. Looking back, you can easily make out the Menai Straits and the great, green spread of land behind. After crossing the pass and its two standing stones, the route descends into the pretty village of Rowen and continues north on minor roads back towards Conwy and its castle walls.

OTHER ROUTES NEARBY

Lon Las Menai & Lon Eifion is a popular tarmacked cycle route from Caernarfon to Bryncir (north-east of Porthmadog) which runs alongside the Welsh Highland Railway for almost 27 kilometres. On nearby Anglesey, Lon Las Cefni is a flat, scenic trail that links Llyn Cefni reservoir with Newborough Forest; the forest also has some easy mountain biking trails on sandy forestry tracks.

BIKE SHOPS AND HIRE

· East End Cycles, Colwyn Bay.
T: 01492 533 834

L–R: *Carneddau ponies above Penmaenmawr; the Smallest House in Great Britain; Great Orme seen from Little Ormes Head* © RK.

17 THE TRIBAN TRAIL

INTRODUCTION
Sandwiched between Eryri (Snowdonia) and the Welsh border, the Clwydian Range Area of Outstanding Natural Beauty (AONB) forms an unmistakeable chain of smooth, rounded, heather-clad hills above the Vale of Clwyd. The hills are crowned with the highest concentration of Iron Age hillforts in Europe, while the Mold Gold Cape – one of the most astonishing relics ever discovered in Wales – was found nearby in 1833. Moel Famau is the AONB's highest hill at 554 metres and towers over the historic town of Ruthin (Rhuthun). There are a number of purpose-built mountain biking trails to enjoy at Coed Llandegla, while the Denbigh Moors (Mynydd Hiraethog) are home to the sprawling Clocaenog Forest and two large artificial lakes: Llyn Brenig and Alwen Reservoir.

ROUTE OVERVIEW
The Triban Trail was first launched back in 2014 as one of the flagship developments of the North Wales Cycling Centre of Excellence project. The challenging route focuses on three key areas – the Clwydian Range, Llyn Brenig and Coed Llandegla – and uses a number of new permissive bridleways that were created especially for the project. Trail highlights include the roller-coaster traverse of Llantysilio Mountain, the wonderfully elevated tracks around Ffrith Mountain and Moel Famau, and the sinuous Two Lakes Cycle Trail. Note that in the summer a number of sections on the original Triban Trail become overgrown and unrideable. The original loop has been included for comparison, but this route offers a close alternative which can be ridden all year round.

Riding on Llantysilio Mountain © RK.

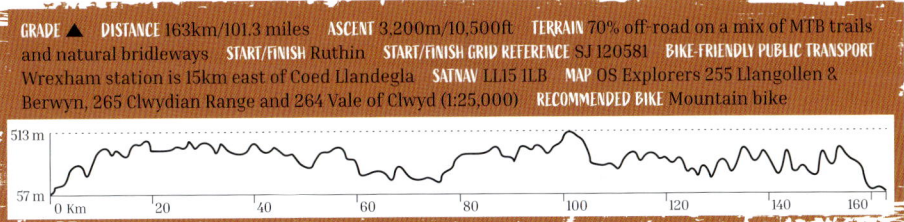

GRADE ▲ DISTANCE 163km/101.3 miles ASCENT 3,200m/10,500ft TERRAIN 70% off-road on a mix of MTB trails and natural bridleways START/FINISH Ruthin START/FINISH GRID REFERENCE SJ 120581 BIKE-FRIENDLY PUBLIC TRANSPORT Wrexham station is 15km east of Coed Llandegla SATNAV LL15 1LB MAP OS Explorers 255 Llangollen & Berwyn, 265 Clwydian Range and 264 Vale of Clwyd (1:25,000) RECOMMENDED BIKE Mountain bike

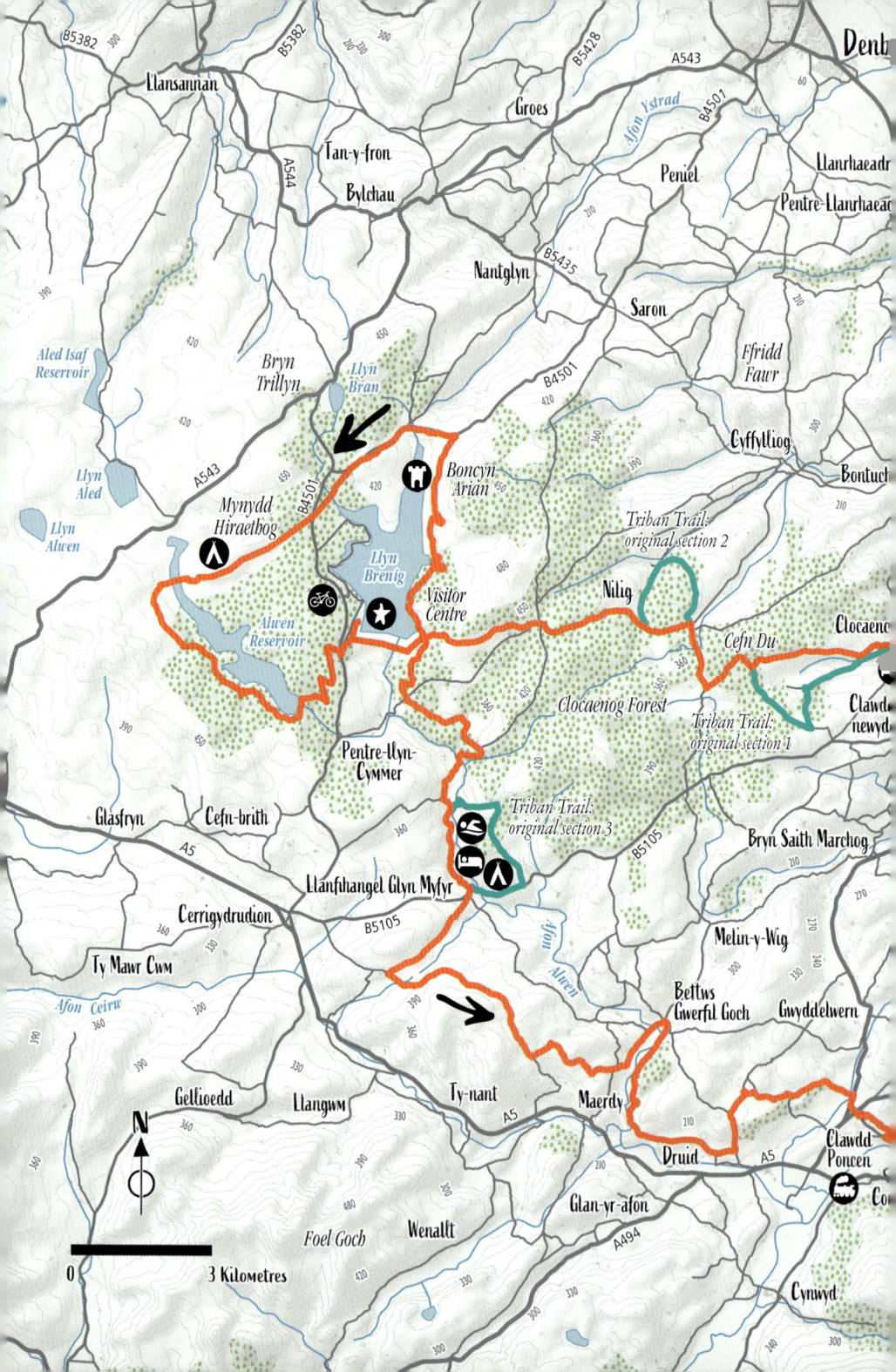

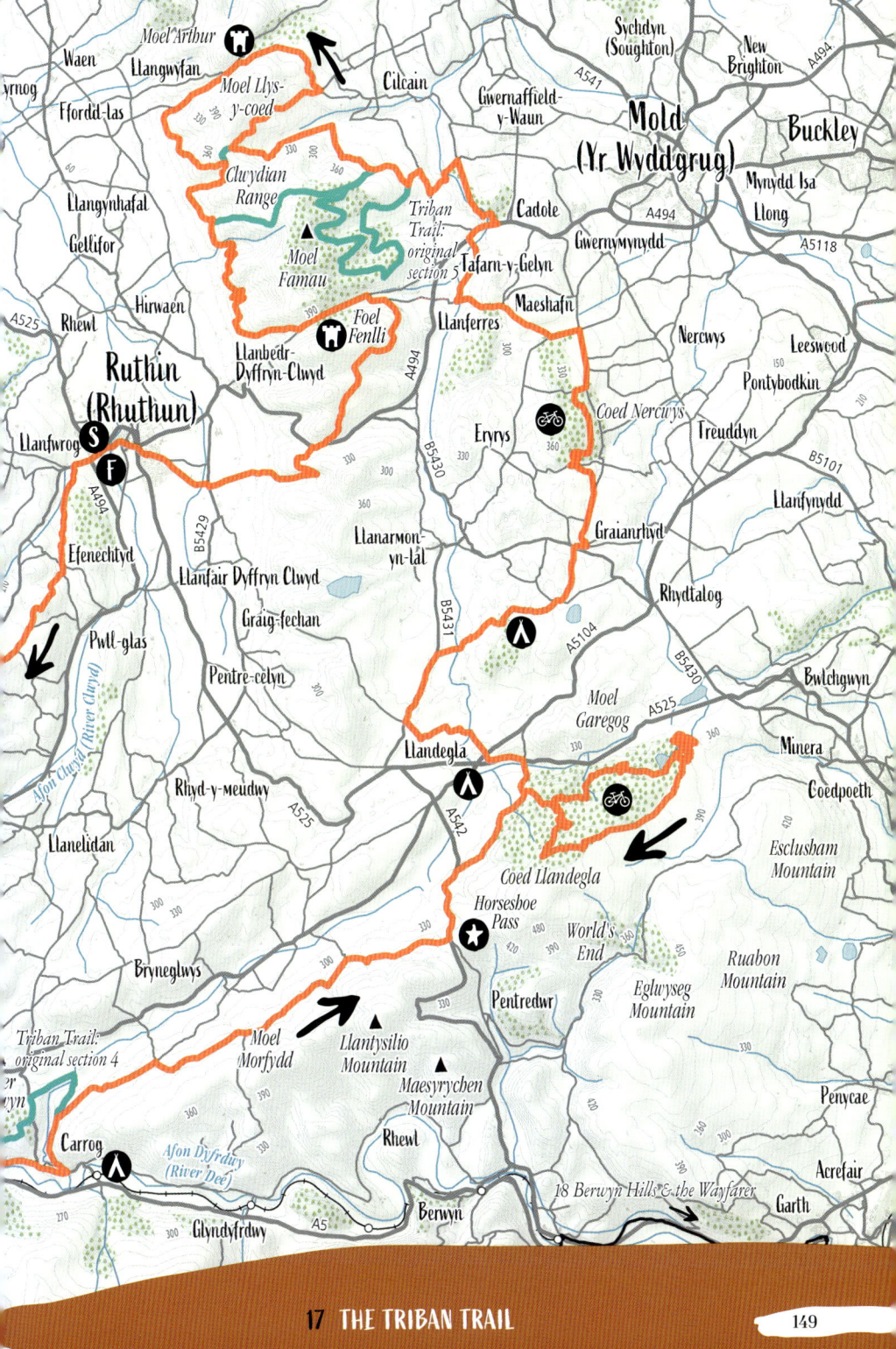

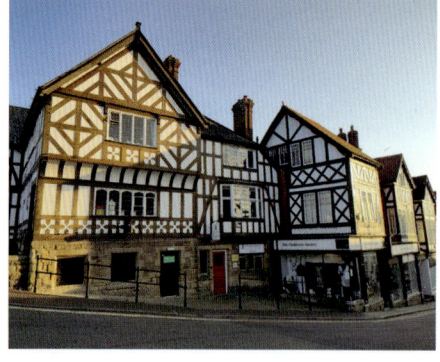

THE ROUTE

It's late evening, and the sun has almost set. Curled up in a bivvy bag, the Vale of Clwyd sprawls below in the last of the light. Smoke from a faraway chimney has started to spread across the valley floor, staying low as it drifts unhurriedly across the patchwork fields and chequered hedgerows. To the west, the familiar skyline of Eryri is easy to make out, Tryfan's jagged crest silhouetted against a red glow on the horizon.

Between 2011 and 2014, Dŵr Cymru (Welsh Water) and Conwy County Borough Council teamed up to deliver the North Wales Cycling Centre of Excellence scheme, a three-year partnership project that aimed to 'create an area nationally renowned as an outstanding, all year round destination for cycling and outdoor activities'. Amongst other improvements, the project resulted in a number of new permissive bridleways and some excellent new cycle trails that were built around the new bike hub at Llyn Brenig Visitor Centre. The Triban Trail was one of the flagship developments of the project – a multi-day route designed to showcase the quality riding on offer in North East Wales, although it has somewhat faded into obscurity since its launch. It turns out the trail makes a great bikepacking route though – challenging, varied and incredibly scenic. The route described here sticks closely to the original trail, with only some minor tweaks to ensure that it is rideable all year round.

Although you could start anywhere along the route, the historic town of Ruthin makes a great base. It is full of beautiful, old black-and-white-timbered houses clustered around an unusual hilltop square, including Nantclwyd y Dre, Wales's oldest dated timbered townhouse. Nearby, the Myddelton Arms is a famous Dutch-style building with seven dormer windows that face out of its huge sloping roof, known as the 'eyes of Ruthin'. Down the hill, Ruthin Castle is a huge, red-stoned mansion built on the site of a 13th-century castle which once survived a revolt by Owain Glyndŵr, as well as an 11-week siege during the English Civil War.

Leaving Ruthin, the opening leg of the route heads west through Clocaenog Forest to reach Llyn Brenig reservoir. The roads and gravel tracks through the forest are lined with

NAVIGATION

This route is not waymarked. However, there are reassuring 'gateway' signs at the start of each of the three main sections – Ruthin, Llyn Brenig and Coed Llandegla; look out for wooden posts topped with a green pyramid. The new permissive bridleways on the eastern side of Moel Famau Country Park are clearly signed with blue circular signs containing a white arrow and a horseshoe. At Llyn Brenig, the route first follows the waymarked Brenig Trail before the Two Lakes Cycle Trail logo appears closer to Alwen Reservoir.

WHEN TO RIDE

The purpose-built trails at Coed Llandegla and around Llyn Brenig and Alwen Reservoir hold up well throughout the year. The Moel Famau permissive bridleways, however, are predominantly grass based and are tough enough in the dry. The trail network at Coed Llandegla is closed to the public when the car park is locked. Check opening times at: www.oneplanetadventure.com

L–R: *Descending off Moel Dywyll © RK; Alwen Reservoir footbridge © RK; the Two Lakes Trail, Llyn Brenig © RK; Ruthin's historic black and white buildings; easy riding on Mwdwl-eithin.*

WARNINGS
Much of the route is exposed with little shelter, apart from short stretches in the forestry plantations. Look out for walkers that share the multi-user trails at Alwen Reservoir and Coed Nercwys.

WATER
There are a number of accessible streams and rivers en route, and more pubs and cafes than you might expect in rural Wales.

FOOD AND DRINK
- Llyn Brenig Lakeside Cafe, Llyn Brenig. T: 01490 420 463
- The Crown Inn & Campsite, Llanfihangel Glyn Myfyr. T: 01490 420 209
- Rhug Estate Farm Shop, Rhug. T: 01490 411 100
- The Grouse Inn, Carrog. T: 01490 430 272
- Ponderosa Cafe, Horseshoe Pass. T: 01978 790 307
- OnePlanet Adventure Cafe, Coed Llandegla. T: 01978 751 656
- Llandegla Community Shop & Cafe, Llandegla. T: 01978 790 604
- Caffi Florence, Loggerheads Country Park. T: 01352 810 397

Ruthin also has plenty of amenities to choose from.

ACCOMMODATION
- Hafod Hall Glamping & Camping, Alwen Reservoir. T: 01690 770 441
- The Crown Inn & Campsite, Llanfihangel Glyn Myfyr. T: 01490 420 209
- Station Campsite, Carrog. T: 01490 430 237
- Llyn Rhys Campsite, Llandegla. T: 01978 790 627
- Allt-Gymbyd Caravan Park, Llandegla. T: 01824 780 958
- The Old Rectory, Clocaenog. T: 01824 750 740

bilberry bushes and are well sheltered from the elements, although it means that the reservoir stays hidden until you are virtually at the water's edge.

Here, the route joins the Two Lakes Cycle Trail which circumnavigates both Llyn Brenig and Alwen Reservoir. The area around the reservoirs is covered in prehistoric monuments including a Bronze Age ring cairn and a burial mound known as Boncyn Arian; both are right next to the trail. The trail itself doesn't start off particularly promising. It follows a wide gravel track along the edge of Llyn Brenig past Hafoty Siôn Llwyd, but at the northern end of the reservoir it joins a new purpose-built cycle path that misses out the busy main road. A narrow slate path cuts through the heather and peat like it's been part of the landscape for years. After circumnavigating the two reservoirs, the trail finishes at Llyn Brenig Visitor Centre with its newly extended cafe and bike hub overlooking the water.

Heading south, the route follows the Afon Alwen down to Llanfihangel Glyn Myfyr. The village has a great pub with its own idyllic campsite right on the riverbank; just upstream, a number of shingle banks and deep river bends are perfect for swimming.

Past Corwen and Carrog, the grassy northern slopes of Llantysilio Mountain (Moel Morfydd) deliver some superb singletrack through the bracken and heather. The route works its way east on a long, linear bridleway, dipping in and out of small cwms and passing several disused quarries to reach the Horseshoe Pass (Bwlch Oernant).

At Coed Llandegla, the Triban Trail loops through the forest

on the popular purpose-built trails. There is a very steep climb on the Offa's Dyke Path to access the trail network, before the route joins a blue-graded section of woodland singletrack to reach the large trail centre cafe and bike workshop. From here, there are a number of fun trails to choose from – both the blue- and red-graded trails are straightforward, even on a loaded bike.

Once past Loggerheads Country Park, the Triban Trail tackles its last challenge – a demanding circumnavigation of Moel Famau ('Mother Mountain') and its neighbouring peaks. Moel Famau is the highest peak in the Clwydian Range and the prominent ruins on its summit are the remains of the Jubilee Tower – a once-huge stone obelisk built in 1810 to celebrate the jubilee of King George III, only to be destroyed in a violent storm 50 years later; just the base remains. The area has benefited hugely from a number of cycling initiatives over the years: the Ride the Clwyds project was the first of its kind in Wales that worked to map, improve and promote a range of natural trails in the area, while more recently the North Wales Cycling Centre of Excellence partnership project has continued to improve and expand the trail network. The riding is wonderfully scenic and there is some excellent singletrack under Ffrith Mountain, but the permissive bridleway along the western slopes of Moel Famau is grassy, indistinct and extremely tough going on a loaded bike. Consider taking the shortcut over the shoulder of Moel Dywyll to miss out the furthest section of the loop if needed. After a stiff climb up to Bwlch Penbarra, the route follows a grassy bridleway around Fron Hen, Moel Eithenin and Moel Gwy before dropping back down into Ruthin.

OTHER ROUTES NEARBY

Ride North Wales (www.ridenorthwales.co.uk) has a huge library of routes to choose from around North Wales. The site is a merger of the popular Ride the Clwyds and Ride Hiraethog sites.

BIKE SHOPS AND HIRE

- OnePlanet Adventure, Coed Llandegla Forest. T: 01978 751 656
- Llyn Brenig Cycle Hire, Llyn Brenig Visitor Centre. T: 01490 389 227
- Cellar Cycles, Ruthin. T: 01824 707 133
- RL's Cycle Repairs, Ruthin. T: 07435 655 405

L–R: *Varied riding on Llantysilio Mountain © RK; sunset over the Vale of Clwyd; the Eyes of Ruthin.*

18 BERWYN HILLS & THE WAYFARER

INTRODUCTION
Known as the gateway to North Wales, the Dee Valley lies just to the west of the border near Wrexham. Much of the valley is now part of the Clwydian Range Area of Oustanding Natural Beauty (AONB) after its boundaries were extended in 2011, including the spectacular Eglwyseg escarpment which towers above some of Wales's most iconic heritage sites. The valley is home to the ruins of Castell Dinas Brân, Valle Crucis Abbey and Chirk Castle, as well as the Llangollen Canal and Pontcysyllte Aqueduct (a UNESCO World Heritage Site). Further south, the Berwyns' exposed, heather-clad hills provide a buffer against neighbouring Eryri (Snowdonia) National Park and are positively empty in comparison.

ROUTE OVERVIEW
No one has written more compellingly about the appeal of the Berwyn Hills or encouraged so many cyclists to follow in his footsteps than cycling journalist Walter MacGregor Robinson, better known simply as 'Wayfarer'. This route is inspired by his memorable crossing of Pen Bwlch Llandrillo during a snowy weekend in March 1919, as well as the evocative article he wrote of the undertaking a couple of weeks later. Starting in Chirk, the loop is bookended by some easy cycling on the Llangollen Canal towpath with the added excitement of two dizzyingly high aqueducts to cross. The bulk of the route, however, takes you on an extended tour of the Berwyns, linking the classic Wayfarer off-road loop with old drove roads and quiet lanes around the beautiful Ceiriog Valley. There is little singletrack to be had, but rugged Welsh bridleways don't get much more scenic than this.

Views of the Berwyn Hills on the Upper Ceiriog Way © RK.

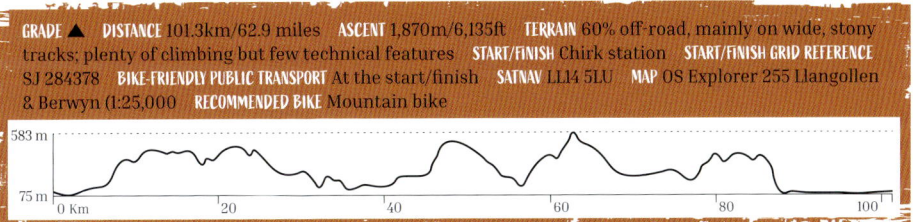

GRADE ▲ **DISTANCE** 101.3km/62.9 miles **ASCENT** 1,870m/6,135ft **TERRAIN** 60% off-road, mainly on wide, stony tracks; plenty of climbing but few technical features **START/FINISH** Chirk station **START/FINISH GRID REFERENCE** SJ 284378 **BIKE-FRIENDLY PUBLIC TRANSPORT** At the start/finish **SATNAV** LL14 5LU **MAP** OS Explorer 255 Llangollen & Berwyn (1:25,000) **RECOMMENDED BIKE** Mountain bike

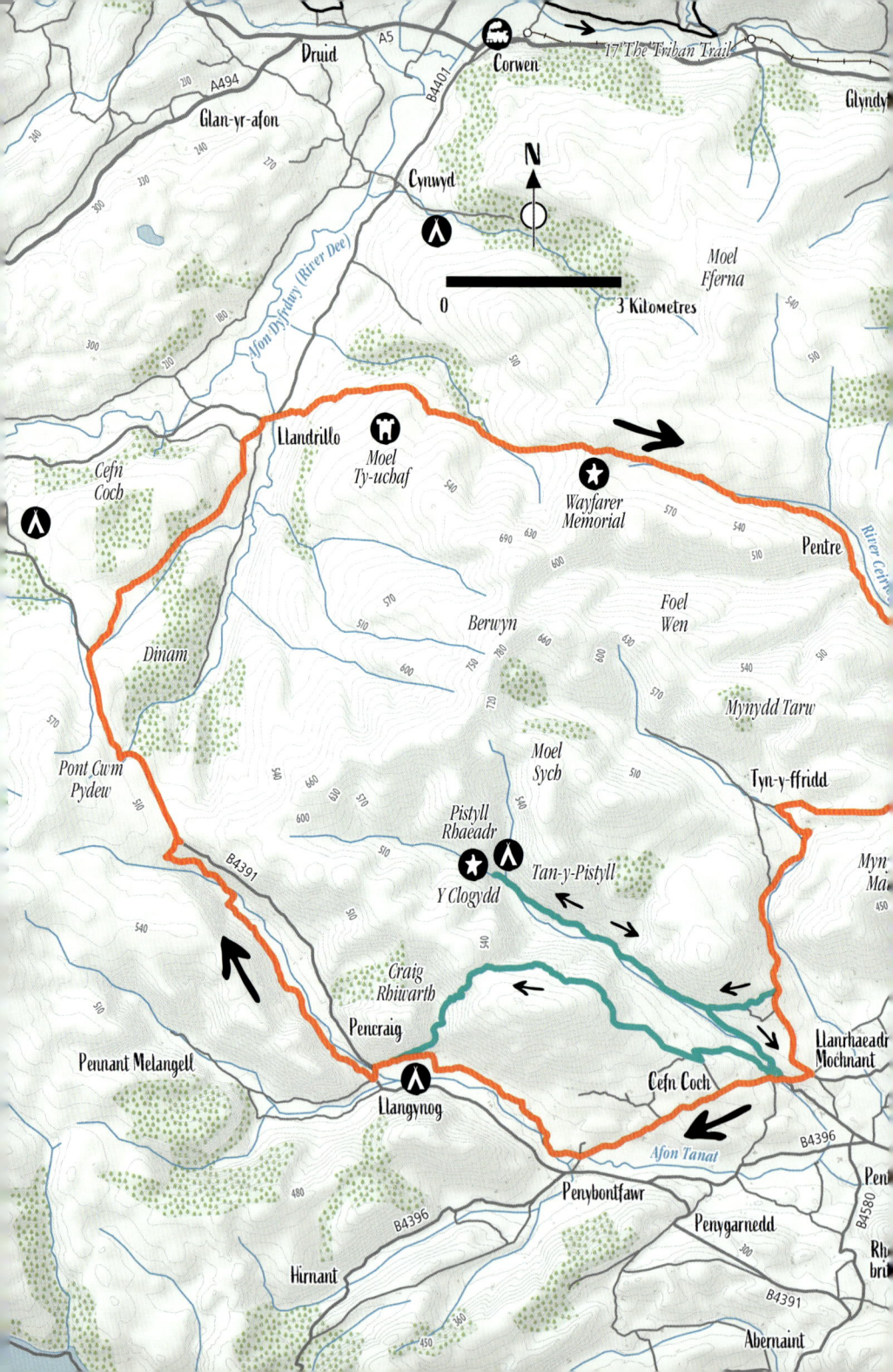

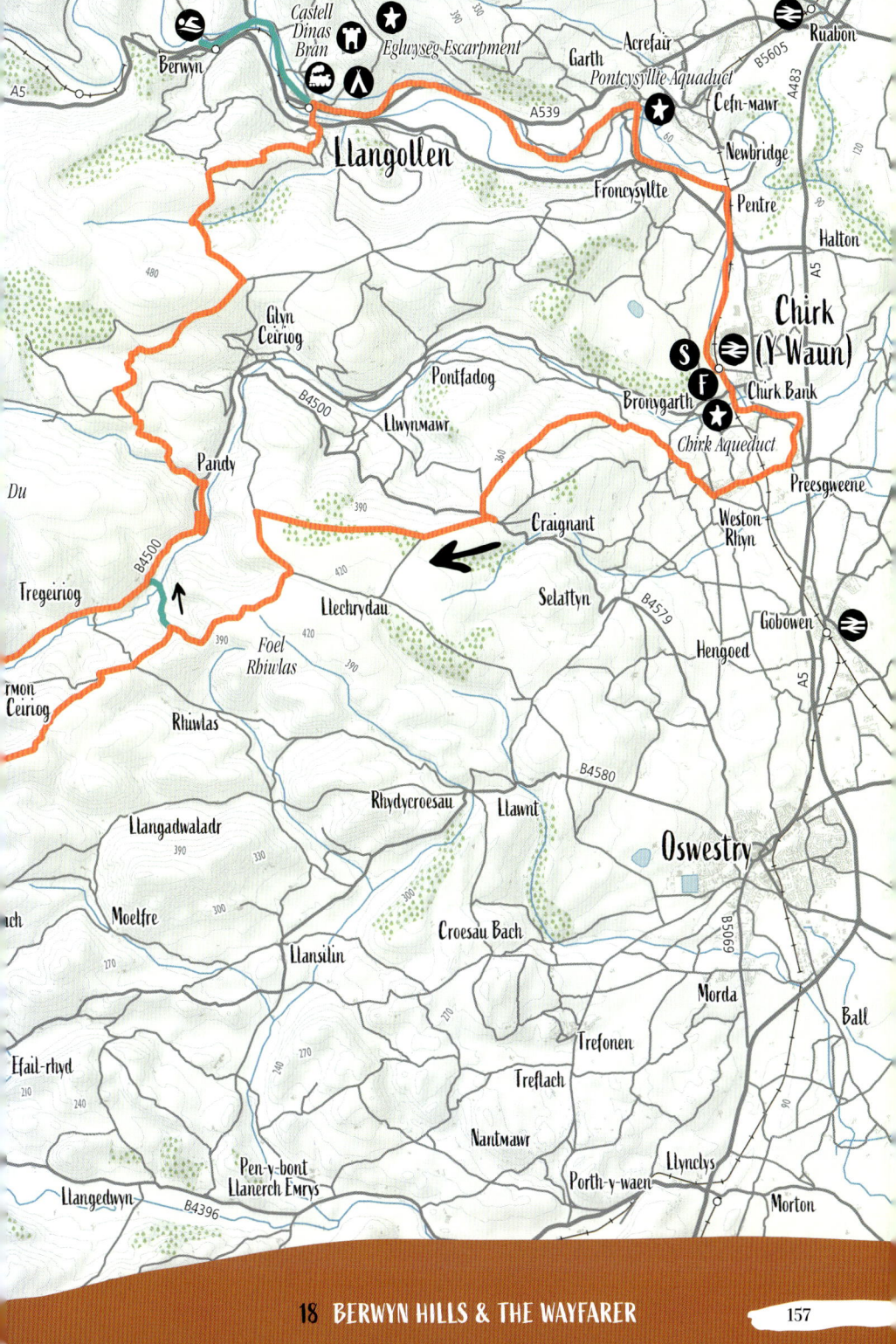

18 BERWYN HILLS & THE WAYFARER

THE ROUTE

'And is this cycling? ... Some of the way over the mountains was ridden, but for the most part it was a walking expedition ... though I am almost a "one-pastime man", I fling wide the boundaries of that pastime and include whatever is incidental thereto. Some of the best of cycling would be missed if one always had to be in the saddle or on a hard road.'
W.M. Robinson, *'Over The Top'* (1919)

The cycling journalist Walter MacGregor Robinson, known to many simply by his pen name Wayfarer, was one of the pioneers of rough-stuff cycling in the UK. His wildly popular talks, articles and lantern-slide lectures in the 1920s and 1930s inspired generations of cyclists to get off the beaten track, especially in the aftermath of World War I. One of Wayfarer's best-known articles, 'Over The Top', was published in *Cycling* magazine in 1919; over a hundred years later, his account of the challenging cycling trip over the Berwyn Hills with two friends from the Anfield Bicycle Club still manages to capture that heady combination of trepidation and excitement that comes with any bikepacking trip. This route follows in Wayfarer's footsteps and pays tribute to that famous crossing.

Leaving the station in Chirk (Y Waun), the route almost immediately follows the canal towpath over Chirk Aqueduct. It's an exciting start to the loop, crossing high above the Afon Ceiriog. After a flat few kilometres along the river and on quiet lanes, the route climbs steeply out of the valley on the Llwybr Ceiriog Trail and crosses through the earthworks of Offa's Dyke.

Further west, the little village of Llanrhaeadr-ym-Mochnant marks the start of two recommended optional detours on the route. Pistyll Rhaeadr ('Spring of the Waterfall') is one of Wales's most spectacular waterfalls, dropping in a series of vertical plunges down a 70-metre cliff face. It is well worth a visit if you have time: take the dead-end road up the valley alongside the Afon Rhaeadr to reach the restaurant, tearoom and waterfall walks (free entry). There is also an optional detour around Glan-hafon to ride the brilliant Nant Ddial switchback descent: a steep ribbon of singletrack that drops into the Tanat Valley through grassy open-access land, beech

NAVIGATION

The start of the bridleway up Cwm Rhirweirth (SJ 032286) has been diverted up the footpath instead due to flood damage. Follow the tarmacked driveway up to the farm and then take the footpath across fields to rejoin the bridleway. The optional singletrack descent down by the side of Nant Ddial is indistinct and grassy to begin with, and then becomes very steep in places. Riders who detour to see Pistyll Rhaeadr can take a steep bridleway out of the valley and over Glan-hafon to connect with the Nant Ddial descent.

WHEN TO RIDE

This route mainly uses rock-based tracks which hold up fairly well throughout the year, although they are badly rutted in places due to off-road vehicle traffic. The Wayfarer crossing over the Berwyn Hills has a number of boggy sections on the eastern side: the worst bits are covered with wooden railway sleepers, but there are still some deep puddles to contend with. The annual Llangollen International Music Eisteddfod is held in early July, and the canal towpaths and aqueducts can get very busy in the summer, especially at weekends.

L–R: *Chirk Aqueduct; RSF 'Wayfarer' memorial; the Eglwyseg escarpment © RK; glamping near Llandrillo; the track up to Pen Bwlch Llandrillo; swimming at Horseshoe Falls.*

WARNINGS

This route crosses two narrow and exposed aqueducts on the Llangollen Canal with unguarded drops. Please dismount and walk along the towpath with your bike on the water side. There is also one unlit tunnel just before you reach Chirk: Whitehouse tunnel is 175 metres long and the towpath is just wide enough for handlebars. Avoid swimming directly below the weir at Horseshoe Falls due to the dangerous currents.

WATER

The rivers en route are not the easiest to access. Fill up in the pubs (check opening times) or carry what you need.

FOOD AND DRINK

- The Hand, Llanarmon Dyffryn Ceiriog. T: 01691 600 666
- The West Arms, Llanarmon Dyffryn Ceiriog. T: 01691 600 665
- SPAR, Llanrheadr. T: 01691 780 095
- Tan-y-Pistyll Cafe, Pistyll Rhaeadr. T: 01691 780 392
- The Stores, Llandrillo (mornings only). T: 01490 440 279
- Plas Newydd Tearoom, Llangollen. T: 01978 862 834
- Butty & Sweet Cafe Boat, Trevor Basin, Llangollen. T: 07743 056 174
- Caffi Wilfa, Chirk. T: 01691 770 492

Pontcysyllte Aqueduct © RK.

woods and loose piles of slate scree that crunch and clatter wonderfully under bike wheels. It is a slog to get to, however, and there is plenty of climbing to come on the route.

The village of Llandrillo lies on the western side of the Berwyns and marks the start of the Wayfarer climb over Pen Bwlch Llandrillo. In *The Drovers' Roads of Wales* (1977), Fay Godwin and Shirley Toulson write that this track was originally known as the 'Maid's Path', as it was the path that girls used to take at harvest time to look for work in the next valley. It was late March, though, when Wayfarer and his two companions set off over the Berwyn Hills, 'to scale the lofty and rugged barrier which lay between us and the Valley of the Dee', and they had to contend with deep snow and blizzards on the way.

Climbing out of Llandrillo, the route embarks on a re-enactment of the famous pass-storming, albeit in reverse. The rough track follows an old drove road up through a tree-lined holloway, between high drystone walls, and then over exposed grass moorland for eight remote kilometres to reach the pass.

In 1957, The Rough-Stuff Fellowship installed a memorial stone at the top of the pass to mark Wayfarer's famous crossing. There is now a replacement metal plaque after the original was damaged, along with a solid steel box nearby with a visitor's book inside.

Leaving the pass, the route descends on a long, drawn-out track through the heather. On the way, it passes an old, dilapidated shooting hut and rumbles over a causeway of wooden railway sleepers before dropping down to Llanarmon Dyffryn Ceiriog. The tiny village boasts two excellent pubs that were used for centuries as a stopping point for drovers on their way to England. The Hand Hotel was used as both a farm and inn until

the early 20th century, while the West Arms Hotel is even older, dating back to 1570. With its low ceilings, uneven flagstones and a roaring fire in the winter, it is easy to picture the three cyclists relaxing here over a hundred years ago as they 'supped and yarned' together the night before their famous crossing.

The final section of the route turns its attention to the Dee Valley and follows a number of high-level, scenic lanes north towards Llangollen. Just before the route begins its descent into the valley, the Eglwyseg escarpment suddenly appears over the rise. It is impossible to miss: towering limestone cliffs and scree sweep across the steep slopes in pale, defined bands of rock, curving around the mountainside in a series of enormous, exposed ledges. Further down, you can just make out the atmospheric ruins of Castell Dinas Brân (free entry) below.

Crossing over the River Dee, the route joins the Llangollen Canal towpath all the way back to Chirk. If you have time, take a detour along the canal to find some fantastic swimming spots near Horseshoe Falls, or visit Valle Crucis Abbey (£) and the ninth-century Pillar of Eliseg (free) slightly further afield. The highlight of the route's finale, though, is Pontcysyllte Aqueduct. Built by Thomas Telford over 200 years ago, it is the highest navigable aqueduct in the world. It spans the Dee Valley on 18 hollow arches and contains some unusual ingredients, including ox blood mixed into the cement to add strength and Welsh flannel used with tar to help seal the troughs. As you walk your bike across the vertiginous towpath, it is easy to see why it is nicknamed the 'stream in the sky'; colourful canal boats and paddleboarders drift past in the cast-iron trough, floating 40 metres above the ground with only a foot-high rim separating them from an unguarded drop on the opposite side.

ACCOMMODATION
- Berwyn Camping, Bwlch y Safn.
  T: 07799 735 177
- Felin Uchaf Camping, Cynwyd.
  T: 07787 717 370
- Henstent Park Camping, Pentre (seasonal). T: 01691 860 479
- Wern Isaf Farm Camping, Llangollen.
  T: 01978 860 632
- Abbey Farm Caravan Park, Llangollen.
  T: 01978 861 297
- Tan-y-Pistyll Camping, Pistyll Rhaeadr (annual membership required).
  T: 01691 780 392

OTHER ROUTES NEARBY
The route follows part of the Llwybr Ceiriog Trail and the Upper Ceiriog Way, two circular routes originally devised for horse riders and marked on 1:25,000-scale OS maps. Revolution Bike Park in Llangynog has had to close for the foreseeable future due to Japanese larch disease.

BIKE SHOPS AND HIRE
- Drosi Bikes, Llangollen.
  T: 07396 658 501
- Dee Valley Bicycle Workshop, Llangollen
  – www.deevalleybicycleworkshop.co.uk

Vertebrate Publishing
The UK's number one publisher of cycling guidebooks

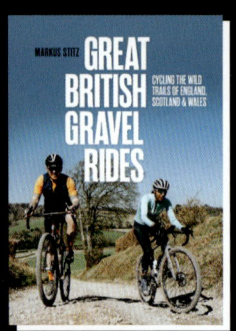
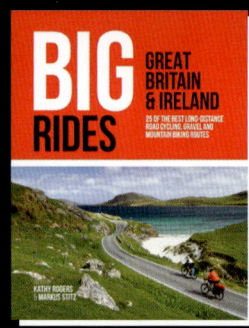
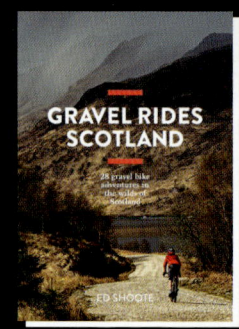
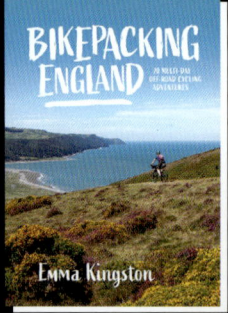
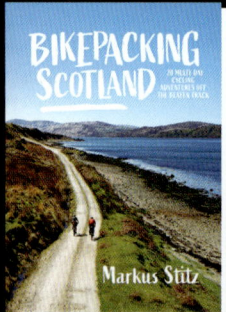

Available from bookshops or direct
Sign up to our newsletter to save 25%

www.adventurebooks.com